Great Americans Speak on the Meaning of History

If we are to know America...
we must understand this social revolution.
We must know why forty million people
left their settled lives
to start new ones in a strange land.
We must know what they did here—
how they met the new land and how it met
them and, most important,
we must know what these things mean for
the present and for the future.

JOHN F. KENNEDY

A plant partakes of the character of
the soil in which it grows. You are a plant
that is conscious, that thinks.
You must study your soil—which is your country
—in order that you may be able to draw its
strength up into your own strength. It will pay
you to do so. You will understand your own
problems better and solve them more easily, if
you have studied America's problems
and done something toward their solution.

DWIGHT D. EISENHOWER

My debt to history is one which cannot be calculated. I know of no other motivation which so accounts for my awakening interest as a young lad in the principles of leadership and government.... I know that the one great external influence which, more than anything else, nourished and sustained that interest in government and public service was the endless reading of history which I began as a boy and which I have kept up ever since.

HARRY TRUMAN

The unparalleled rise of America has not been the result of riches in lands, forests, or mines; it sprang from the ideas and ideals which liberated minds and stimulated the spirits of men. In those ideas and ideals are the soul of the people. No American can review this vast pageant of progress without confidence and faith, without courage, strength, and resolution for the future.

HERBERT HOOVER

Kennedy: "A Nation of Immigrants," New York, 1959
Eisenhower: Reader's Digest, October, 1948
Truman: "Memoirs," © 1955, Time Inc.
Hoover: 150th anniversary address, Yorktown, Va., October 19, 1931

INTRODUCTION

This is the second volume of the encyclopedia of famous Americans — and the final volume of *The Golden Book History of the United States*. It contains the biographies of more than 250 distinguished men and women with names running from M to Z. As in Volume 11, each name is followed by a section in *italic* type which lists the person's vital statistics—where and when he was born, where and when he died, and the dates of the various major events of his life. Below that, in Roman type like this, is the story of his greatest achievements, of the deeds that earned him his place among the 500 most famous Americans.

Note: Difficult names are followed by a pronunciation guide. Accented syllables are in *italic,* for example, *Wash*-ing-ton.

Remember, after reading a biography, to refer back to the period of the person's life in the first ten volumes of your *Golden Book History*. Here you will see the pattern of events surrounding his achievements, the pattern of events his own life may have helped to change. For our famous Americans are those who have lived—and made—our history.

THE GOLDEN BOOK

HISTORY of the UNITED STATES

FAMOUS AMERICANS

VOLUME 12 M to Z

by **IRVING WERSTEIN**

PETER LACEY, *Art Research*

HERBERT J. SANBORN, *Art Research*

GOLDEN PRESS  **NEW YORK**

Library of Congress Catalog Card Number: 63-9433
© Copyright 1963 by Golden Press, Inc. and The Ridge Press, Inc.   Printed in the U.S.A. by Western Printing and Lithographing Co.

Douglas MacArthur

M

MacARTHUR, DOUGLAS

Born: Jan. 26, 1880, Little Rock, Ark. Graduated, West Point (1903). Served in Philippines (1903-04, 1922-25) and Japan (1905-06). Aide-de-camp to President Theodore Roosevelt (1906-07). Army general staff (1913-15, 1916-17). Commander, 42nd (Rainbow) Division, France (1917-18). Superintendent, U.S. Military Academy (1919-22). Brigadier general (1920). Major general (1925). Chief of staff, U.S. Army (1930-35). Director, Philippine Commonwealth national defense (1935-37). Retired (1937).

The most brilliant chapters of General MacArthur's military career came when he was recalled to duty after a lifetime of service. In July, 1941, as the threat of World War II hung over the U.S., the sixty-one-year-old MacArthur was made lieutenant general and commander of U.S. Forces in the Far East.

After Japan invaded the Philippines (1941), MacArthur conducted a fighting retreat through Bataan peninsula to Corregidor, an island fortress in Manila Bay. Ordered to Australia, MacArthur left the Philippines with the promise, "I shall return."

As Supreme Allied Commander in the Southwest Pacific (1942), MacArthur led campaigns against Japan in New Guinea and in the liberation of the Philippines. He was made a five-star general in 1944, and accepted the Japanese surrender that ended World War II aboard the battleship *Missouri* (1945). After the war, he was occupation commander of Japan (1945-51) and gave far-reaching assistance in rebuilding the shattered nation.

When Communist forces invaded South Korea (1950), MacArthur was made head of the United Nations forces there. His long service ended unhappily in April, 1951, when he was relieved of his command by President Truman after a disagreement on policy.

McCLELLAN, GEORGE BRINTON

Born: Dec. 3, 1826, Philadelphia, Pa. Died: Oct. 29, 1885, Orange, N.J. Graduated, West Point (1846). Served in Mexican War. Assistant instructor in military engineering, West Point (1848-51). U.S. observer, Crimean War (1855). Vice-president, Illinois Central R.R. (1858) and president (1860).

For the period of a year, George McClellan was the chief soldier of the Union army and the chief hope for a Northern victory. Having enjoyed a success against the Confederates in western Va. in the early months of the Civil War, he was given a major command after the Union disaster at Bull Run, Va. (July, 1861). In November, he replaced old General Winfield Scott as commander in chief of the Union armies. He devoted his efforts to training and equipping the Army of the Potomac, was slow and cautious about moving into action. He finally launched an attack against the Confed-

Cyrus McCormick

erate capital at Richmond, Va. (the Peninsular Campaign, March to August, 1862), but was defeated in the Battles of the Seven Days and forced to retreat. In September, 1862, he stopped Lee at Antietam, Md., but failed to follow up his advantage against Lee's troops. In November, he was relieved of his command.

"Little Mac" ran unsuccessfully against Lincoln in the presidential election of 1864. He later served as governor of N.J. (1878-81).

McCORMICK, CYRUS HALL

Born: Feb. 15, 1809, Rockbridge Co., Va. Died: May 13, 1884, Chicago, Ill.

Cyrus McCormick designed and built the first successful machine for reaping grain. He set up a plant in Chicago, Ill., to manufacture it (1847), and within a few years had developed a nationwide business.

The McCormick reaper was the beginning of labor-saving agricultural machinery in the U.S. And its inventor also introduced new marketing methods, such as installment-plan buying, field trials, and advertising testimonials from satisfied users.

MacDOWELL, EDWARD ALEXANDER

Born: Dec. 18, 1861, and Died: Jan. 24, 1908, New York City.

Edward MacDowell studied piano and composition in Europe, and was a professor of music at Columbia from 1896-1904. Thereafter he gave his full time to composition. His works include four piano sonatas and such orchestral tone poems as *Hamlet, Ophelia, Lancelot and Elaine, The Saracens,* and *The Fair Alda.* He also wrote many songs and piano pieces, among them the well-known "To a Wild Rose."

The MacDowell colony for composers, artists, and writers at Peterborough, N.H., was founded in his memory, and according to his plan, by his widow, Marian Nevins MacDowell. There talented artists congregate every summer for undisturbed work.

McDOWELL, IRVIN

Born: Oct. 15, 1818, Columbus, O. Died: May 4, 1885, San Francisco, Cal. Graduated, West Point (1838). Fought in the Mexican War (1845-48). Major general (1872).

On May 14, 1861, a month after the start of the Civil War, Irvin McDowell was appointed brigadier general and given command of the Union troops which later became the Army of the Potomac. He led them at the First Battle of Bull Run, Va. (July, 1861), which ended in a defeat for the North. McDowell was replaced as commander of the Army of the Potomac by General George B. McClellan, but retained command of a corps of Union troops. In August, 1862, he again met defeat at Second Bull Run and never again held a field command.

McGUFFEY, WILLIAM HOLMES

Born: Sept. 23, 1800, near Claysville, Pa. Died: May 4, 1873, Charlottesville, Va. Graduated, Washington Coll., Md. (1826). Professor of languages, philosophy, and philology, Miami U., O. (1826-36). President, Cincinnati Coll., O. (1836-39). President, Ohio U. (1839-43). Professor, Woodward Coll., O. (1843-45) and the U. of Virginia (1845-73).

William McGuffey was the author of America's most famous series of schoolbooks: *McGuffey Eclectic Readers.* There were six books, published between the years 1836-57. They were used by schools in thirty-seven states, went

Edward MacDowell

William H. McGuffey

through numerous editions, and sold an estimated 122,000,000 copies.

McGuffey Readers were a mixture of entertaining literature, self-improvement themes, and patriotic and moral essays.

McKAY, DONALD

Born: Sept. 4, 1810, Shelbourne, Nova Scotia. Died: Sept. 20, 1880, Hamilton, Mass.

Donald McKay was a designer and builder of ships, particularly the swift and beautiful clipper ships that for a few decades were the finest merchant vessels to sail the seas. McKay came to the U.S. as a ship's carpenter, opened his first shipyard in 1841, and by 1845 was established in Boston, Mass. He built some of the largest wooden ships of his time, and many clippers, such as the famous *Flying Cloud*, which set a record sailing from Boston to San Francisco in 1851.

By 1873, iron steamships had ended the age of sail and McKay closed his yard forever.

McKINLEY, WILLIAM

Born: Jan. 29, 1843, Niles, O. Died: Sept. 14, 1901, Buffalo, N.Y. Studied law, Albany, N.Y. Admitted to O. bar (1867). Practiced in Canton, O. Elected, prosecuting attorney, Stark Co., O. (1869). Congressman (1876-81, 1883-90). Governor of O. (1891-95).

When he was eighteen years old, William McKinley fought with the Union army in several major battles, including South Mountain and Antietam, Md. He entered the army (1861) as a private and was mustered out a major (1865). After serving as Republican congressman and governor of O., McKinley became the nation's twenty-fourth President (1897-1901) by beating William Jennings Bryan.

The U.S. gained new territory during McKinley's term of office. As a result of the Spanish-American War (April-July, 1898), Spain gave up the Philippines, Guam, and Puerto Rico. Hawaii was annexed in July, 1898.

McKinley again defeated Bryan in the election of 1900, but was shot by Leon Czolgosz, an anarchist, during a visit to the Pan-American Exposition in Buffalo, N.Y. (September 6, 1901). The President died eight days later and was succeeded by Theodore Roosevelt.

McMILLAN, EDWIN MATTISON

Born: Sept. 18, 1907, Redondo Beach, Cal. Graduated, California Institute of Technology, B.S. (1928), M.S. (1929); Ph.D., Princeton (1932).

Edwin Mattison McMillan, a nuclear physicist, is director of the U. of California radiation laboratory.

In 1940, McMillan discovered neptunium (Element 93) and plutonium (Element 94), which proved essential in producing the atomic bomb. He also worked on the construction of the first cyclotron and other atom-smashing machinery. During World War II, he developed radar devices and equipment for detecting submerged submarines (sonar).

McMillan was a winner of the Nobel prize in chemistry (with Glenn Seaborg) (1951).

MADISON, JAMES

Born: Mar. 16, 1751, Port Conway, Va. Died: June 28, 1836, Montpelier, Va. Graduated, Coll. of New Jersey (Princeton) (1771). Mem-

ber, Continental Congress (1780-83). Member, Constitutional Convention (1787). Co-author (with Hamilton and Jay) of the Federalist papers (1787-88). U.S. congressman (1789-97).

As much as any man, and more than most, James Madison deserves to be called the "Father of the Constitution." He never missed a session of the convention, debated his points with wisdom and distinction, and compiled the best and most complete account of the proceedings. He then wrote twenty-eight of the *Federalist* papers to explain the new Constitution and enlist support for it. And as a delegate to the House of Representatives from Va., he introduced at the first U.S. Congress a series of constitutional amendments, ten of which were passed and became the Bill of Rights.

He served as President Jefferson's Secretary of State (1801-09) and was himself fourth President of the U.S. (1809-13). He defeated DeWitt Clinton to win re-election (1813-17). On his retirement from politics in 1817, Madison helped Jefferson establish the U. of Virginia, and served as rector (1826-36).

Madison's wife, Dorothea (Dolly) Payne Todd (1768-1849), made her own place in history. A woman of great social charm and grace, she acted swiftly to save the famous Peale portrait of George Washington and other White House valuables when the British invaded and burned the capital during the War of 1812.

MAHAN, ALFRED THAYER

Born: Sept. 27, 1840, West Point, N.Y. Died: Dec. 1, 1914, Washington, D.C. Graduated, U.S. Naval Academy (1859). Captain (1885). President, Naval War Coll., R.I. (1866-89, 1892-93). Retired (1896). Advanced to rank of rear admiral (1906).

Admiral Mahan (Ma-*han*) wrote The Influence of Sea Power Upon History, 1660-1783, a classic study of the impact of naval policy on international events. Mahan argued that navies decided wars and that how a navy was used politically was as important as how it was used militarily. His work later affected both the writing of naval history and the policies of wartime powers.

MANN, HORACE

Born: May 4, 1796, Franklin, Mass. Died: Aug. 2, 1859, Yellow Springs, O. Graduated, Brown U. (1819). Attorney at Dedham, Mass., and Boston (1823-37). Mass. legislature (1827-33) and Mass. senate (1833-37).

As secretary of the first state board of education in Mass. (1837-48), Horace Mann overhauled and modernized the entire educational system. He established at Lexington, Mass., the first state teachers' training school in the U.S. (1839). He aroused public interest in educa-

Dolly Madison

Horace Mann

tion, collected statistics to show people what the educational problems were, and he fought to get better schoolhouses and equipment, more pay for teachers, and improved programs.

He resigned to accept the congressional seat vacated by the death of John Quincy Adams (1848-53), and proved a vigorous opponent of slavery during his term in the legislature. Defeated for re-election, he served from 1853-59 as first president of Antioch Coll., O.

MARIN, JOHN

Born: Dec. 23, 1872, Rutherford, N.J. Died: Oct. 1, 1953, Addison, Me.

John Marin was a great water-colorist, perhaps best known for his seascapes. He studied at the Pennsylvania Academy of Fine Arts (1900), went abroad in 1905, and was first shown in New York in 1909. His work, in which the influences of Chinese painting and postimpressionism are combined, is owned by many museums and private collections.

MARION, FRANCIS

Born: About 1732, Georgetown, S.C. Died: Feb. 28, 1795, near Eutaw, S.C. Elected, S.C. provincial congress (1775); state senate (1781, 1782, 1784).

When Camden, S.C., fell to the British (1780) during the American Revolution, a troop of cavalry commanded by Francis Marion became the chief force opposing the redcoats in S.C. and in much of the South. Resorting to guerrilla tactics, Marion harassed the foe, cutting communications, raiding camps, ambushing troop columns, burning supply dumps, and raiding enemy outposts. When pursued, Marion and his men vanished into the swamps. These elusive, hit-and-run tactics earned him the title of the "Swamp Fox."

MARKHAM, EDWIN

Born: Apr. 23, 1852, Oregon City, Ore. Died: Mar. 7, 1940, Staten Island, N.Y.

Edwin Markham quit teaching and devoted himself to writing and lecturing after he had

George C. Marshall

gained fame as a poet through a single work, "The Man With the Hoe" (1899). Later collections of his works include *Lincoln and Other Poems* (1901), *Shoes of Happiness, and Other Poems* (1915), *Gates of Paradise* (1920).

MARSHALL, GEORGE CATLETT

Born: Dec. 31, 1880, Uniontown, Pa. Died: Oct. 17, 1959, Washington, D.C. Graduated, Virginia Military Institute (1901). A.E.F. (1917-18). Aide-de-camp to General John J. Pershing (1919-24). General and chief of staff, U.S. Army (1939-45). Appointed general of the army (1944).

George C. Marshall was a distinguished soldier who was equally well-versed in the arts of peace. As chairman of the Joint Chiefs of Staff (1941-45), he was the principal American military strategist of World War II. Shortly after the war's end, he was appointed U.S. ambassador to China, and then (1947-49) President Truman's Secretary of State. In this role he proposed and carried out a plan to assist the economic recovery of war-torn Europe—the so-called "Marshall Plan." He also served (1950-51) as Secretary of Defense. In 1953 he was awarded the Nobel peace prize.

MARSHALL, JOHN

Born: Sept. 24, 1755, Germantown (now Midland), Va. Died: July 6, 1835, Philadelphia, Pa. Received private education. Served in Revolutionary War (1775-79). Attended law lectures, William and Mary Coll. (1780). Practiced law, Richmond, Va. (from 1783). Active in Va. state government (1782-95). U.S. congressman (1799-1800). Secretary of State under President John Adams (1800-01).

John Marshall was appointed Chief Justice of the U.S. Supreme Court by President John Adams in January, 1801. Although there had been three prior Chief Justices, the Court's position was weak and vague. In the thirty-four years of Marshall's term, however, during the administrations of five Presidents, the Court was raised to a position of power equal to that of the national executive and legislative branches of the government. Many of the basic interpretations of the Constitution also were made by the "Marshall Court."

MARTIN, GLENN L.

Born: Jan. 17, 1886, Macksburg, Ia. Died: Dec. 4, 1955, Baltimore, Md.

A pioneer pilot and airplane manufacturer, Glenn Martin held many flying records for speed, endurance, and altitude between 1909-16. He built one of the first airplane factories in the U.S. (1909) and received the first government order for aircraft (1913). In 1945 he founded the Glenn L. Martin Coll. of Engineering and Aeronautical Sciences at the U. of Maryland.

MASON, GEORGE

Born: 1725, Northern Neck, Va. Died: Oct. 7, 1792, Gunston Hall, Va. Member, Va. House of Burgesses (1759). Va. legislature (1776-80). Delegate to Constitutional Convention (1787).

George Mason was one of the wealthiest landowners in Va. and a liberal-minded patriot. He wrote most of Va.'s constitution (1776) and its famous Declaration of Rights, which was used as a model by several other colonies and is echoed in part in the Declaration of Independence. Mason took an active part in drafting the U.S. Constitution, but did not sign it. He did not approve of its provisions concerning slaves or its lack of protection for civil rights. When it was ratified by Va. in spite of his opposition, he drafted proposals for debate in the new U.S. Congress which were the basis for the Bill of Rights.

MASTERS, EDGAR LEE

Born: Aug. 23, 1869, Garnett, Kan. Died: Mar. 5, 1950, Melrose Park, Pa.

Edgar Lee Masters was the author of the *Spoon River Anthology* (1915). This was a volume of epitaphs in free verse, a revealing picture of the life of a small American town in terms of the triumphs and tragedies of some of its citizens. He also wrote several biographies.

MAURY, MATTHEW FONTAINE

Born: Jan. 14, 1806, near Fredericksburg, Va. Died: Feb. 1, 1873, Lexington, Va. Superintendent, Depot of Charts and Instruments, later the Naval Observatory (1842-61). Professor of meteorology at Virginia Military Institute (1868-73).

Matthew Maury was the foremost oceanographer of his time. He wrote the first great textbook of modern oceanography, *The Physical Geography of the Sea* (1855). It was based on years of research on the winds, currents, and geography of the bottom of the major oceans. He was the first man to describe the Gulf Stream, to chart the Atlantic Ocean bottom between the U.S. and England, and to mark out the fastest routes across the oceans.

Herman Melville

H. L. Mencken

MAYO, CHARLES HORACE

Born: July 19, 1865, Rochester, Minn. Died: May 26, 1939, Chicago, Ill. Graduated, Northwestern U., M.D. (1888). Served, U.S. Army Medical Corps, World War I.

MAYO, WILLIAM JAMES

Born: June 29, 1861, Le Sueur, Minn. Died: July 28, 1939, Rochester, Minn. Graduated, U. of Michigan, M.D. (1884). Served, U.S. Army Medical Corps, World War I.

The Mayo brothers, Charles and William, were doctor sons of a distinguished surgeon, Dr. William Worrall Mayo (1820-1911), known as the "Pioneer Surgeon of the Northwest." Upon completing their medical education, Charles and William joined their father's practice in Rochester, Minn. The brothers originated new methods for operations, William in the field of abdominal surgery, Charles in surgery of the thyroid glands.

The small clinic opened by their father in 1889 was eventually built by the brothers into the internationally famed Mayo Clinic. It includes practitioners, surgeons, and medical technicians—some 200 specialist doctors united in a co-operative enterprise. In 1915, the brothers established the Mayo Foundation for Medical Education and Research as a branch of the U. of Minnesota.

MEADE, GEORGE GORDON

Born: Dec. 31, 1815, Cadiz, Spain. Died: Nov. 6, 1872, Philadelphia, Pa. Graduated, West Point (1835). Brigadier general of volunteers (1861); major general (1864).

After distinguishing himself in action in the Battles of Second Bull Run, Fredericksburg, and Chancellorsville, Va., and Antietam, Md., General Meade was given command of the Army of the Potomac (1863). A few days later, he led it to victory in the most important single engagement of the Civil War—the Battle of Gettysburg (July 1-3, 1863).

MELVILLE, HERMAN

Born: Aug. 1, 1819, and Died: Sept. 28, 1891, New York City.

Herman Melville had a wildly adventurous life before becoming an author. He went to work at fifteen to help support his poverty-stricken family. He held jobs as a clerk, farmer, and teacher until 1837, when he went to sea. He sailed on the whaler *Acushnet* (1841-42), jumped ship, and took refuge among cannibal tribesmen of the Marquesas Islands. Rescued by another whaler, he landed at Tahiti, made his way to Hawaii, and returned to the U.S. (1844) by enlisting as a crewman on the American frigate *United States*.

His first novels, *Typee* (1846), *Omoo* (1847),

Mardi (1849), *Redburn* (1849), and *White-Jacket* (1850), were based on his own adventures, and met with success upon publication.

He moved to Pittsfield, Mass. (1850), where he began a long friendship with Nathaniel Hawthorne. Hawthorne encouraged Melville to write *Moby Dick* (1851). Although now regarded as a classic and Melville's masterpiece, the book was a critical and financial failure when first published. Melville's later works were either ignored or attacked by the critics and the public.

He moved to New York City, worked as a customs inspector (1866-85), and lived in obscurity while continuing to write. A remarkable novelette, *Billy Budd, Foretopman*, written shortly before his death, was found among Melville's papers and published in 1924.

MENCKEN, HENRY LOUIS

Born: Sept. 12, 1880, and Died: Jan. 29, 1956, Baltimore, Md. Newspaperman on Baltimore papers (from 1899). Co-editor, Smart Set *magazine (1914-23). Co-founder,* American Mercury *magazine (1924); editor (1925-33).*

H. L. Mencken was a newspaperman, a literary critic, and a social commentator. In sharp and amusing language he attacked American attitudes, manners, and customs that he felt were stuffy, ignorant, and tasteless. Aided by his longtime friend, drama critic George Jean Nathan, he filled two magazines for two decades with fresh ideas, opinions, and judgments on the arts and American life. His most noteworthy work, *The American Language* (1918), is a serious study of the American idiom.

MERGENTHALER, OTTMAR

Born: May 11, 1854, Hachtel, Germany. Died: Oct. 28, 1899, Baltimore, Md.

Ottmar Mergenthaler was the inventor of the Linotype typesetting machine (1884). Trained as a watchmaker, he came to the U.S. in 1872. His first job was with the U.S. government in Washington, D.C.

At that time, printing was done with handset metal type; each letter of a word, or sentence, or book, had to be picked from a font (type box) and patiently placed in proper order. Mergenthaler's machine, with its typewriter-like keyboard, enabled an entire line of type (Linotype) to be set at one time. The New York *Tribune*, attracted by the idea of faster setting, installed the first Linotype in 1886.

MICHELSON, ALBERT ABRAHAM

Born: Dec. 19, 1852, Strelno, Prussia. Died: May 9, 1931, Pasadena, Cal. Brought to U.S. (1854). Graduated, U.S. Naval Academy (1873). Instructor, physics and chemistry, U.S. Naval Academy (1875-77). Taught physics, Case School of Applied Sciences, O. (1883-89) and at Clark U., Mass. (1889-92). Head of physics department at U. of Chicago (1892-1929).

Albert Michelson was a physicist who measured the speed of light with the highest degree of accuracy ever achieved. His work paved the way for Einstein's later discovery of the theory of relativity. Michelson was awarded the Nobel prize in physics (1907), the first American scientist ever to be so honored.

MILLAY, EDNA ST. VINCENT

Born: Feb. 22, 1892, Rockland, Me. Died: Oct. 19, 1950, Austerlitz, N.Y. Graduated, Vassar (1917).

Edna St. Vincent Millay (Mill-*ay*) won recognition as a poet at the age of twenty with her long poem, "Renascence." Her later works include *A Few Figs from Thistles* (1920), the Pulitzer-prize-winning poem, "The Ballad of the Harp-Weaver" (1923), *Wine from These Grapes* (1934), and *Conversation at Midnight* (1937). She wrote dramatic verse plays for radio, and the libretto of Deems Taylor's opera, *The King's Henchman* (produced, 1927). She was a master of the difficult, fourteen-line sonnet form.

MILLIKAN, ROBERT ANDREWS

Born: Mar. 22, 1868, Morrison, Ill. Died: Dec. 19, 1953, Pasadena, Cal. Graduated, Oberlin Coll., O. (1891); Columbia, Ph.D. (1895). Taught physics, U. of Chicago, Ill. (1896-1921).

Chairman, executive committee, California Institute of Technology (1921-45).

Robert Millikan, one of America's most distinguished physicists, was the first to identify the electron and measure its negative electrical charge. For this work he received the Nobel prize in physics in 1923. He also did important work on cosmic rays and X rays.

MITCHELL, WILLIAM LENDRUM

Born: Dec. 29, 1879, Nice, France. Died: Feb. 19, 1936, New York City. Graduated, George Washington U. (1898). Infantry private, Spanish-American War (1898). Served in Philippines and Mexico. General staff, U.S. Army (1913). Commander, air services, A.E.F. (1917-18). Brigadier general (1920). Director, military aviation (1920-25).

"Billy" Mitchell, the youngest officer ever appointed to the army general staff, sacrificed a brilliant military career to win acceptance for air power. As director of military aviation after World War I, he called for a large and independent air force. He argued that airplanes would be a major factor in another war, and sank "unsinkable" battleships with aerial bombs to prove it. He finally accused the War and Navy Departments of "almost treasonable administration of national defense," and was court-martialed for insubordination (disobedience). He was sentenced to a five-year suspension without pay or allowances. Mitchell resigned (1926) and continued his barrage of criticism as a civilian.

In 1942, six years after his death, the U.S. was involved in a second world war that air power did much to win. By a congressional resolution, Mitchell's court-martial verdict was set aside, and he was posthumously promoted to major general.

"Billy" Mitchell

MITSCHER, MARC ANDREW

Born: Jan. 26, 1887, and Died: Feb. 3, 1947, Hillsboro, Wis. Commander, 8th Fleet (Jan., 1946). Commander in chief, Atlantic Fleet (Sept., 1946).

In 1919, Marc Mitscher piloted the U.S. Navy aircraft that made the first transoceanic flight from Newfoundland to the Azores. He also served tours of duty on the early aircraft carriers *Langley* and *Wright*.

During World War II, he was skipper of the U.S.S. *Hornet* when Jimmy Doolittle's B-25's were launched for their epic air raid on Japan (1942). And he was commander of the huge Task Force 58 which dealt punishing blows to the Japanese navy in 1944-45.

MONROE, JAMES

Born: Apr. 28, 1758, Westmoreland Co., Va. Died: July 4, 1831, New York City. Attended William and Mary (1774-76). Left to join Continental army. Studied law under Thomas Jefferson (1780-83). Member, Continental Congress (1783-86). U.S. senator (1790-94). Minister to France (1794-96). Governor of Va. (1799-1802, 1811). Helped arrange Louisiana Purchase (1803). Minister to Great Britain (1803-07). Secretary of State (1811-17). Secretary of War (1814-15).

James Monroe's two terms as fifth President of the U.S. were known as "the era of good feeling" (1817-25). The nation was at peace. Strife between its political parties—the Federalists and the Democratic-Republicans—had quieted down. Settlers were already moving into the Middle West, many into states carved from the Louisiana Purchase Monroe had helped to arrange. Florida was acquired from Spain (1819), boundary disputes with Canada were settled, and border forts were abandoned.

Monroe's political and diplomatic career owed much to his close friendship with Jefferson, his old law teacher. And Monroe was unswervingly loyal to Jefferson's principles that government should not be centralized and all-powerful, but should respect states' rights.

He is best remembered for the statement of U.S. foreign policy that bears his name. The Monroe Doctrine was announced in a message to Congress in 1823, and was in large part the work of Secretary of State John Quincy Adams. Basically, it told Europe to keep hands off the Americas—that the United States would not stand by while any European nation tried to colonize, or interfere with the government of, any part of the western hemisphere.

Dwight L. Moody

MOODY, DWIGHT LYMAN

Born: Feb. 5, 1837, and Died: Dec. 22, 1899, Northfield, Mass.

Dwight L. Moody was a successful shoe salesman who gave up the business world in 1861 and devoted himself to religious missionary work. He met Ira D. Sankey (1840-1908), an evangelist and hymn singer, in 1870. Together they conducted tremendously popular revival meetings, featuring Moody's sermons and Sankey's hymns, throughout the 1880s.

MOORE, CLEMENT CLARKE

Born: July 15, 1779, New York City. Died: July 10, 1863, Newport, R.I.

Clement Moore was a graduate of Columbia (1798), a Biblical scholar, and a professor of Oriental and Greek literature. He is best remembered, however, for a poem he wrote for his children (1822) and called, *Visit from St. Nicholas*. Its first line goes:" 'Twas the night before Christmas...."

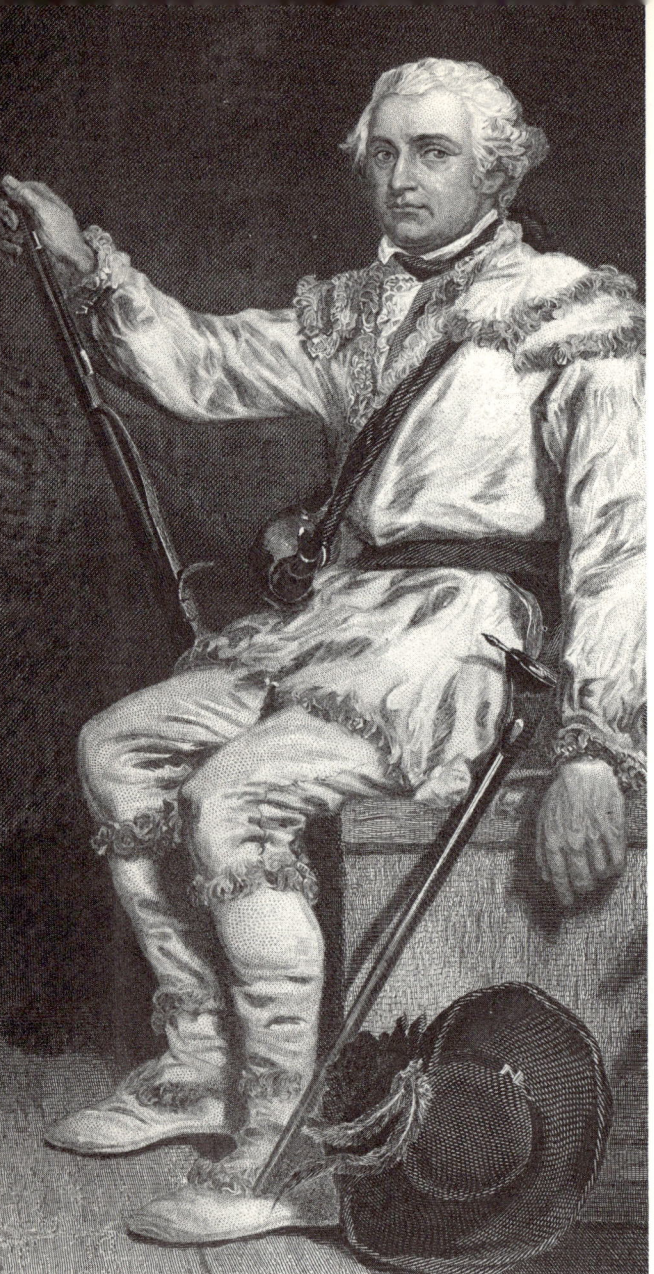

Daniel Morgan

MOORE, MARIANNE

Born: 1887, St. Louis, Mo. Graduated, Bryn Mawr (1909). Editor of Dial *(1925-29).*

While teaching stenography, and later while working in the New York Public Library, Marianne Moore was writing poetry and sending it to an English magazine, *Egoist*. Her work was witty and imaginative, and the *Egoist* was a willing publisher.

In 1921 her friends selected poems from the magazine without her knowledge and published her first volume of collected verse, *Poetry*. Her writings constitute a major contribution to American poetry. Among her collections are: *Observations* (1924), *Selected Poems* (1935) (with an introduction by T. S. Eliot), *What Are Years* (1941), *Nevertheless* (1944), and *A Marianne Moore Reader* (1961).

MORGAN, DANIEL

Born: July 6, 1736, Hunterdon Co., N.J. Died: July 6, 1802, Winchester, Va. U.S. congressman (1797-99).

Daniel Morgan served under Benedict Arnold during the ill-fated American expedition to seize Quebec (1775). Morgan, who commanded a company of riflemen, led his men into the city but was forced to surrender (December 31, 1775). Released from captivity (November, 1776), he organized a body of 500 Va. riflemen whose accurate marksmanship helped defeat General Burgoyne at the Battle of Saratoga, N.Y. (1777). In 1781, his sharpshooters won another victory over the British army at Cowpens, S.C.

After the war, Morgan commanded the Va. militia that put down the Whiskey Rebellion (1794) in western Pa.

MORGAN, JOHN PIERPONT

Born: Apr. 17, 1837, Hartford, Conn. Died: Mar. 31, 1913, Rome, Italy. Educated in Switzerland and Germany. Entered J. S. Morgan banking house, London (1856). Arrived New York City (1857). Associated with various banking firms. Founded J. P. Morgan and Co. (1895).

J. P. Morgan was the financial giant of 19th-century America. The son of international banker, Junius Spencer Morgan (1813-90), he was himself a power by the time of the Civil War. He eventually pyramided the family fortunes into a gigantic complex of banks, insurance companies, railroads, and industrial corporations. In 1901 he formed U.S. Steel Corp., the nation's first billion-dollar corporation.

The House of Morgan continued through his son, also John Pierpont (1867-1943), who helped the Allied governments finance the first world war.

The elder Morgan amassed a $50,000,000 collection of art, most of which is now in New York's Metropolitan Museum of Art. The remainder, together with an extraordinary collection of rare manuscripts, first editions, and other valuable literary materials, is in the Morgan Library, New York City.

MORGAN, THOMAS HUNT

Born: Sept. 25, 1866, Lexington, Ky. Died: Dec. 4, 1945, Pasadena, Cal. Graduated, State Coll. of Kentucky (1886); John Hopkins, Ph.D. (1890). Professor of biology, Bryn Mawr (1891-1904). Professor of experimental zoology, Columbia (1904-28). Director, biological science, California Institute of Technology (1928-45).

Thomas Hunt Morgan was a zoologist who pioneered in the science of genetics (the study of heredity, or the way characteristics are passed on from one generation of living things to another). Using the fruit fly, *Drosophila*, Morgan discovered and demonstrated certain laws of heredity. For this he was awarded the Nobel prize in physiology and medicine (1933).

MORLEY, EDWARD WILLIAMS

Born: 1838, Newark, N.J. Died: 1923, Hartford, Conn. Graduated, Williams Coll. (1860). Professor of chemistry, Western Reserve (1869-1908).

Edward Morley was a chemist and physicist. He studied the densities of oxygen and hydrogen, the relative motion of the earth, the speed of light in a magnetic field, the expansion of gases when heated, and how heat is conducted through water vapor.

MORRILL, JUSTIN SMITH

Born: Apr. 14, 1810, Strafford, Vt. Died: Dec. 28, 1898, Washington, D.C. U.S. congressman (1855-67). U.S. senator (1867-98).

Justin Smith Morrill, who spent the remarkable total of forty-three consecutive years in Congress, was the sponsor of the Morrill, or Land-Grant College, Act (1862). Under this provision, government lands were given to states to establish colleges for teaching agriculture and the mechanic arts. The act encouraged the establishment of the many land-grant state institutions in existence today.

MORRIS, GOUVERNEUR

Born: Jan. 31, 1752, and Died: Nov. 6, 1816, Morrisania, N.Y. Graduated, King's Coll. (Columbia) (1768). Practiced law, New York City. Member, N.Y. provincial congress (1775-77). Signer, Articles of Confederation (1775). Member, Continental Congress (1777-78). Assistant minister of finance (1781-85). Delegate, Constitutional Convention (1787). U.S. commissioner to England (1790-91). Minister to France (1792-94). U.S. senator (1800-03). Chairman, Erie Canal Commission (1813-14).

Gouverneur Morris was a wealthy aristocrat who gave a lifetime of service to the American Revolution and the young nation that resulted from it. He was one of the major contributors to the Constitutional Convention. He was a frequent and persuasive debater for a strong central government, and as a member of the Committee of Style wrote much of the final language of the Constitution.

MORRIS, ROBERT

Born: Jan. 31, 1734, near Liverpool, England. Died: May 8, 1806, Philadelphia, Pa. Member, Continental Congress (1776-78). Signer, Declaration of Independence (1776). Superintendent of finance (1781-84). Delegate, Constitutional Convention (1787). U.S. senator (1789-95).

Robert Morris was a wealthy merchant who skillfully arranged the difficult financing of the American Revolution. He raised funds to purchase supplies for Washington's armies, sometimes pledging his personal fortune as credit to get loans for the Continental government. Later, as superintendent of finance under the Articles of Confederation, he arranged a loan with France which made the establishment of the Bank of North America possible. Oddly enough, he died bankrupt, losing his fortune in Western land speculation.

Robert Morris (standing)

MORSE, SAMUEL FINLEY BREESE

Born: Apr. 27, 1791, Charlestown, Mass. Died: Apr. 2, 1872, New York City. Graduated, Yale (1810). Studied art, Royal Academy, London, England; portrait painter (1815-37). A founder and first president, National Academy of Design (1826-42). Professor of painting, New York U. (from 1832).

Samuel Morse had a considerable reputation as a portrait painter when he decided instead to devote himself to developing the magnetic telegraph. For twelve years, he worked on the idea. He had technical assistance from Leonard Gale (1800-83) and Joseph Henry; financial help from Alfred Vail (1807-59) and Ezra Cornell (1807-74), founder of the Western Union Telegraph Co. (1856) and co-founder of Cornell U. (1865).

On May 24, 1844, the practicality of the telegraph was demonstrated to Congress when Morse sent the message, "What hath God

S. F. B. Morse

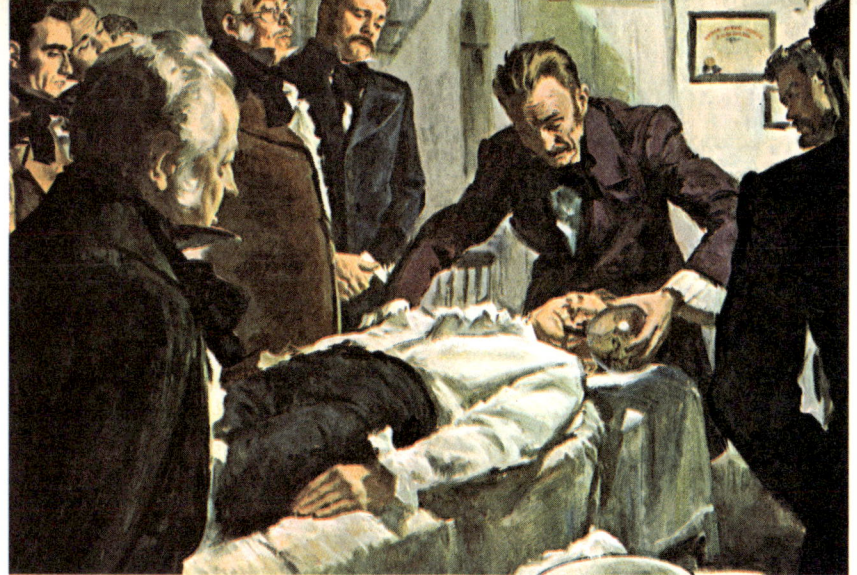
William Morton

wrought!" over newly strung wires from Washington, D.C., to Baltimore (by Morse code).

MORTON, WILLIAM THOMAS GREEN

Born: Aug. 9, 1819, Charlton, Mass. Died: July 15, 1868, New York City. Graduated, Baltimore Coll. of Dental Surgery (1842).

Dr. William Morton was the first man to demonstrate the effectiveness of ether as an anesthetic. At Mass. General Hospital in Boston (October 16, 1846) surgery was performed on a patient anesthetized against pain by Morton's procedure. Credit for this achievement must also be given to Dr. C. W. Long (1815-78), of Ga., who used ether in a similar case four years earlier, but failed to bring it to public attention.

MOULTRIE, WILLIAM

Born: 1730, and Died: Sept. 27, 1805, Charleston, S.C. Brigadier general, Continental army (1776), major general (1782). Governor, S.C. (1785-87, 1794-96). U.S. senator (1787-91).

General Moultrie, a veteran Indian fighter, prevented the British from taking Charleston, S.C., in 1776 by his fierce defense of a small fort on Sullivan's Island (later named Fort Moultrie) in Charleston harbor. When the British finally took the city (1780), Moultrie was taken prisoner. He was exchanged in 1782 and served to the end of the war.

MUIR, JOHN

Born: Apr. 21, 1838, Dunbar, Scotland. Died: Dec. 24, 1914, Los Angeles, Cal. Studied, U. of Wisconsin (1859-63).

John Muir (Mewer), raised on a farm in Wis., had a deep love of nature. Shortly after leaving the U. of Wisconsin, he suffered an accident that threatened to blind him. Because he wanted to study nature while he still could see, Muir traveled through the woodlands and mountains of the Western states and Alaska.

He kept his sight and became one of America's greatest naturalists. It was largely through his efforts that Yosemite (Cal.) and other national parks were established. He also helped bring about conservation laws in the U.S., and was the author of many books about nature.

MURPHY, WILLIAM PARRY

Born: Feb. 6, 1892, Stoughton, Wis. Graduated, Harvard, M.D. (1922), and taught there (1923).

Dr. William Murphy specialized in researching the causes and treatments of such diseases as diabetes and anemia (a disease resulting from the loss of red blood corpuscles). He was a co-winner of the 1934 Nobel prize in medicine and physiology, sharing the award with Dr. George R. Minot (1885-1950) and Dr. George H. Whipple (1878——) for their joint efforts in treating anemia.

Thomas Nast

N

NAST, THOMAS

Born: Sept. 27, 1840, Landau, Bavaria (Germany). Died: Dec. 7, 1902, Guayaquil, Ecuador. U.S. consul to Ecuador (1902).

Thomas Nast was a brilliant political cartoonist whose clever, razor-sharp drawings helped expose and destroy William Marcy "Boss" Tweed (1823-78) of New York City. (Jailed on charges of thievery and corruption, Tweed fled the country, only to be recognized in Spain through Nast's cartoons. He was caught and returned to serve his sentence.)

Nast also originated the country's most familiar political symbols—the Democratic donkey and the Republican elephant.

NATION, CARRY AMELIA

Born: Nov. 25, 1846, Garrard Co., Ky. Died: June 9, 1911, Leavenworth, Kan.

As the head of the Women's Christian Temperance Union (W.C.T.U.), Carry Nation launched a campaign to wipe out saloons (1900). Hatchet in hand, she invaded a Wichita, Kan., saloon, smashing glasses and bottles and beer kegs. The hatchet-wielding made her a famous figure in the U.S.

NIMITZ, CHESTER WILLIAM

Born: Feb. 23, 1885, Fredericksburg, Tex. Graduated, U.S. Naval Academy (1905). Chief of staff, U.S. Submarine Fleet, World War I. Rear admiral (1938). Chief, Bureau of Navigation (1939-41). Admiral (1941). Admiral of the fleet (1944). Chief, naval operations (1945-47).

After the Japanese attack on Pearl Harbor, Chester W. Nimitz was made commander in chief of the Pacific Fleet. Nimitz helped conceive the strategy of "island hopping" to drive the Japanese out of their Pacific strongholds. He launched his offensive at Guadalcanal (August, 1942) and kept attacking through the Solomon Islands, the Bonins, the Marshalls, and the Gilberts.

When Japan surrendered (September, 1945), Nimitz commanded 6,256 ships and 4,847 combat aircraft, the largest naval force in history.

NIXON, RICHARD MILHOUS

Born: Jan. 9, 1913, Yorba Linda, Cal.

As a congressman (1947-51) and U.S. senator (1951-53), Richard Nixon was a leader in the fight against people in government whom he considered to be Communists. Nixon's role in the prosecution and conviction of a State Department official, Alger Hiss, focused national attention on the young senator.

Nixon served as Vice-President under President Dwight D. Eisenhower (1953-61), and was the Republican nominee for President in 1960. He was defeated by John F. Kennedy in a close election.

NORRIS, FRANK

Born: Mar. 5, 1870, Chicago, Ill. Died: Oct. 25, 1902, San Francisco, Cal. Educated, U. of Chicago and Harvard.

Frank Norris began his writing career as a correspondent for the San Francisco *Chronicle* during the Boer War in South Africa (1895). He also covered the Spanish-American War

Carry Nation

(1898) for *McClure's Magazine*. His first and finest novel, *McTeague* (1899), provided a harsh and realistic picture of a man's struggle against the inner force of greed and the outside forces of nature and society. Norris was among the first in American literature to choose more shocking and depressing elements of life for his subjects and to document the problems of the individual in relation to a complex society. Later works, *The Octopus* (1901) and *The Pit* (1903), are in this style.

NORRIS, GEORGE WILLIAM

Born: July 11, 1861, Sandusky Co., O. Died: Sept. 2, 1944, McCook, Neb. Graduated, Northern Indiana Normal School (now Valparaiso U.) (1882). District attorney, Furnas Co., Neb.; district judge (1895-1902). U.S. congressman (1903-13). U.S. senator (1913-43).

Senator George Norris was a ruggedly independent man. Although he served most of his political career as a Republican, his constant disagreements with G.O.P. policy finally caused him to be read out of the party (1936). He continued his course as an Independent, the description that always fitted him best. He opposed President Wilson, World War I, and the Treaty of Versailles. He was strongly in favor of President Franklin Roosevelt's New Deal, and relief for farmers. In the 1930s, he led the successful fight for the Tennessee Valley Authority. He also sponsored (1933) the 20th Amendment which changed the presidential inauguration day from March to January, thereby doing away with the time-wasting "Lame Duck" session of Congress.

Chester W. Nimitz

OLMSTED, FREDERICK LAW

Born: Apr. 26, 1822, Hartford, Conn. Died: Aug. 28, 1903, Waverly, Mass. Named superintendent, Central Park, New York City (1857).

Frederick Law Olmsted was a pioneer in American landscape architecture. He designed Central Park (with Calvert Vaux [1824-95]) and was its first superintendent. His success with this early effort at city planning earned him many commissions from other cities. Between the years 1865-95, he laid out Prospect Park, Brooklyn; Riverside Park, New York City; the Capitol grounds, Washington, D.C.; the park systems of Boston, Hartford, and Louisville; the Chicago World's Fair (1893), and the campuses of Stanford U. and of the U. of California.

O'NEILL, EUGENE GLADSTONE

Born: Oct. 16, 1888, New York City. Died: Nov. 27, 1953, Boston, Mass. Attended Princeton U. (1906-08), Harvard (1914-15).

Eugene Gladstone O'Neill, the son of actor James O'Neill (1849-1920), decided to become a playwright in 1914. He became associated in 1916 with the Provincetown Players who, during the next four years, produced ten of his one-act plays, including *Bound East for Cardiff* and *The Moon of the Caribbees.*

In 1920, *Beyond the Horizon* was produced on Broadway and won the Pulitzer prize. O'Neill also took the award in 1922 for *Anna Christie,* in 1928 for *Strange Interlude,* and posthumously, in 1957, for *Long Day's Journey Into Night*. In addition, he was awarded the Nobel prize for literature (1936).

A brilliant and imaginative dramatist, O'Neill is generally agreed to be America's greatest playwright. Between 1920 and 1933, he wrote: *The Emperor Jones, Diff'rent, The Hairy Ape, All God's Chillun Got Wings, De-*

Eugene O'Neill

Elisha Otis

James Otis

Thomas Paine

sire Under the Elms, The Great God Brown, Lazarus Laughed, Marco Millions, Dynamo, Mourning Becomes Electra, Ah, Wilderness!, and Days Without End.

In 1946 *The Iceman Cometh* was produced, and after his death, *A Moon for the Misbegotten*, *A Touch of the Poet*, and *Long Day's Journey Into Night*.

OTIS, ELISHA GRAVES

Born: Aug. 3, 1811, Halifax, Vt. Died: Apr. 8, 1861, Yonkers, N.Y.

Employed as a master mechanic (1851) at a factory in Yonkers, N.Y., Elisha Otis designed an automatic safety device for elevators. From this he developed the first passenger elevator (1857). His success led him to open a shop at Yonkers for the manufacture of elevators. Known as the Otis Elevator Co., the firm became the largest producer of lifts in the U.S.

OTIS, JAMES

Born: Feb. 5, 1725, West Barnstable, Mass. Died: May 23, 1783, Andover, Mass. Graduated, Harvard (1743). Admitted to Mass. bar (1748). Mass. legislature (from 1761).

James Otis was among the early leaders of the American Revolution. An attorney, he helped direct colonial resistance against various British acts of taxation. He also wrote a pamphlet, *The Rights of the British Colonies Asserted and Proved* (1764), which argued that the crown could not tax the colonists without permitting them the full privileges enjoyed by all Englishmen.

P

PAINE, THOMAS

Born: Jan. 29, 1737, Thetford, England. Died: June 8, 1809, New York City.

Thomas Paine had the rare ability to describe in stirring and encouraging words the meaning of a political upheaval for the people involved in it. A failure at every business venture he ever tried, he was in times of fear, peril, and confusion a clear and inspiring voice. His pamphlet, *Common Sense* (1776), called for a separation from England and helped spur the Declaration of Independence. His series of pamphlets, *The American Crisis*

Francis Parkman

(1776-83), rallied patriots in the dark days of the Revolution. ("These are the times that try men's souls. The summer soldier and the sunshine patriot will, in this crisis, shrink from the service of his country; but he that stands it *now*, deserves the love and thanks of man and woman.")

PARKMAN, FRANCIS

Born: Sept. 16, 1823, Boston, Mass. Died: Nov. 8, 1893, Jamaica Plain, Mass. Graduated, Harvard (1844). Professor, Horticultural School, Harvard (1871-72).

Francis Parkman suffered from a number of physical and mental disorders, including eyesight so weak that it bordered on blindness. But these handicaps did not prevent him from becoming the leading American historian of his time.

His first work, *The California and Oregon Trail* (1849), was the result of two trips he made over the trail from St. Louis. His later works were about the struggle between England and France for control of North America: *Pioneers of France in the New World* (1865), *Count Frontenac and New France Under Louis XIV* (1877), and *Montcalm and Wolfe* (2 vols., 1884).

PARSONS, WILLIAM BARCLAY

Born: Apr. 15, 1859, and Died: May 9, 1932, New York City. Chief engineer, Rapid Transit Commission, New York City (1894-1905).

William Parsons was the civil engineer who built the first sections of the New York City Subway System (1899-1904). He also supervised construction of the East River tunnel, and served as consulting engineer for the Panama Canal (1904-05), chief engineer of the Cape Cod Canal (1905-14), and chairman of the Chicago Transit Commission (1916).

PATTON, GEORGE SMITH, JR.

Born: Nov. 11, 1885, San Gabriel, Cal. Died: Dec. 21, 1945, Frankfort-am-Main, Germany. Graduated, West Point (1909). Aide to General Pershing in Mexico (1916-17), France (1917). Commanded, 2nd Armored Division

(1940); U.S. Forces, Morocco (1942); 2nd Army Corps, Tunisia (1943); 7th Army, Sicily (1943); 3rd Army, Western Europe (1944-45). Promoted to rank of full general (1945).

George Patton—"Old Blood and Guts"—was noted for his pearl-handled pistols, quick temper, and fierce tactics in battle. He was the first officer assigned to the army's tank corps (1917) and by World War II had become one of America's few trained specialists in mechanized warfare. His most brilliant campaign was the swift 3rd Army drive from Normandy, across France, the Rhine, and southern Germany, to Czechoslovakia.

PAULING, LINUS CARL

Born: Feb. 28, 1901, Portland, Ore. Graduated, Oregon State Coll., B.S. (1922); California Institute of Technology, Ph.D. (1925). Professor, chemistry and chairman, division of chemical engineering, California Institute of Technology (from 1931).

One of the world's foremost chemists, Linus Pauling has concentrated his research on the structure of molecules and the chemical bond. In 1954 he was awarded the Nobel prize in chemistry for discoveries in that field.

PEALE, CHARLES WILLSON

Born: Apr. 15, 1741, Queen Anne Co., Md. Died: Feb. 22, 1827, Germantown, Pa. Officer in Revolution at Battles of Trenton and Princeton. Founder, Pennsylvania Academy of Fine Arts (1805).

Charles Peale was renowned as a painter of George Washington, executing some sixty studies of him between 1772-95.

Peale had eleven children, all of whom he named after famous artists. Three of them became painters themselves: Raphael (1774-1825), who specialized in miniatures and still lifes; Rembrandt (1778-1860), noted for historical scenes and life portraits of Washington, Jefferson, and Napoleon; and Titian Ramsay (1799-1885), who, in addition to his work as a painter, was also a naturalist and explorer.

PEARY, ROBERT EDWIN

Born: May 6, 1856, Cresson, Pa. Died: Feb. 20, 1920, Washington, D.C. Graduated, Bowdoin, Me. (1877). U.S. Coast and Geodetic Survey (1879-81). Lieutenant and civil engineer, U.S. Navy (from 1881). Rear admiral (1911).

Robert E. Peary, the first man to reach the

George S. Patton, Jr.

Charles Willson Peale

Robert E. Peary

North Pole, achieved his goal on his fourth try. He began his arctic explorations with voyages to Greenland in 1886 and 1891-92. He then made three attempts at the Pole which failed—the third (1905-06) ending a scant 174 miles from the objective. Success came in 1908-09. Accompanied by a Negro servant, Matthew Henson, and four Eskimos, Peary made the final dash to the Pole by dog sled from Ellesmere Island (April 6, 1909).

Peary's achievement was disputed by Dr. Frederick A. Cook (1865-1940), who claimed he had reached the Pole a year before, on April 21, 1908. After bitter controversy, scientific and geographical experts decided in Peary's favor.

PEIRCE, CHARLES SANDERS

Born: Sept. 10, 1839, Cambridge, Mass. Died: Apr. 19, 1914, Milford, Pa. Graduated, Harvard (1859), M.A. (1862), Sc.B. (1863). U.S. Coast Survey (1861-91). First American delegate to International Geodetic Congress (1877).

Charles Sanders Peirce was a physicist, mathematician, and logician. Although his astronomical observations provided the material for his only book, *Photometric Researches* (1878) Peirce specialized in geodesy (the measurement of vast land areas). He was among the most brilliant men of his day in that field. But Peirce's fame rests on his contributions to scientific methodology and logical thought; his ideas influenced such thinkers as William James, Josiah Royce, and John Dewey.

PENN, WILLIAM

Born: Oct. 14, 1644, London, England. Died: July 30, 1718, Ruscombe, England. Expelled from Oxford for Quaker leanings (1662). Joined Society of Friends. Received grant of territory in what is now Pennsylvania from Charles II (1681).

William Penn founded the colony of Pa. as

a place where men could enjoy religious and political freedom. He received the land from Charles II of England in payment of a debt the king owed Penn's father, Admiral Sir William Penn. Penn visited the grant in 1682, made peace with the Indians, supervised the layout of Philadelphia, and worked out a pattern of government with the colonists. In 1689 he founded a public grammar school which still exists **(Penn Charter)**.

PERKINS, FRANCES

Born: Apr. 10, 1882, Boston, Mass. Graduated, Mt. Holyoke Coll. (1902); Columbia, M.A. (1910). N.Y. Committee on Safety (1912-17). N.Y. State Industrial Board (1923-26), chairman (1926-29).

Frances Perkins, Secretary of Labor (1933-45), was the first woman to hold a cabinet post in the U.S. Through her various government jobs in the state of N.Y., she became an expert in industrial hazards, hygiene, and the working conditions of women. She was an able administrator of the vast Labor Department during a period in which labor's role in U.S. life was vastly increased and was becoming more and more complex.

PERRY, MATTHEW CALBRAITH

Born: Apr. 10, 1794, Newport, R.I. Died: Mar. 4, 1858, New York City. Commodore, U.S. Navy (1841).

As a midshipman, Matthew Calbraith Perry served under his brother, Oliver Hazard Perry,

Matthew C. Perry

in the War of 1812. Matthew was also one of the first naval officers to argue for a steam-powered navy and was commander of the first U.S. Navy steamship, the *Fulton* (1837).

His most notable feat, however, was in the field of diplomacy. In 1853, as the representative of President Millard Fillmore, Perry led a naval squadron into Tokyo Bay to end Japan's centuries of isolation from the western world. He persuaded the Japanese to trade with the U.S., and returned to Japan in 1854 to sign the first commercial treaty between the two countries.

PERRY, OLIVER HAZARD

Born: Aug. 20, 1785, South Kingston, R.I. Died: Aug. 23, 1819, on the Orinoco River, Venezuela. Midshipman, U.S. Navy (1799). Saw service during naval war with France. Served in Tripolitanian War (1802-06) and War of 1812. Captain (1814).

During the spring and summer of 1813, Oliver Hazard Perry, commanding U.S. naval forces on Lake Erie, built a fleet of ten war vessels for those waters. His largest ships were the *Lawrence* and the *Niagara*.

On September 10, 1813, he led them to victory over a British naval squadron in the Battle of Lake Erie, heroically rowing from his flagship, the *Lawrence,* to the *Niagara* in the midst of the heated contest when the *Lawrence* was badly battered. "We have met the **enemy** and they are ours," Perry signaled later. The triumph gave the Americans control of **Lake Erie**, and was one of the decisive actions of the War of 1812.

PERSHING, JOHN JOSEPH

Born: Sept. 13, 1860, Linn Co., Mo. Died: July 15, 1948, Washington, D.C. Graduated, West Point (1886); U. of Nebraska, LL.B. (1893). U.S. military attaché, Tokyo, Japan (1905-06). Pulitzer prize in history (1932) for his book, My Experiences in the World War *(1931).*

As commander in chief of the American Expeditionary Force (A.E.F.) in France, General John J. Pershing was the nation's top soldier

John J. Pershing

of World War I. His troops called him "Black Jack." He was a veteran cavalry officer who had campaigned against the Indians in the Southwest (1886-90), the Spaniards in Cuba (1898), the Moros in the Philippines (1899-1903, 1913), and the bandit leader Francisco "Pancho" Villa in Mexico (1916). He was named general of the armies (1919) and served as army chief of staff (1921-24).

PHILLIPS, WENDELL

Born: Nov. 29, 1811, and Died: Feb. 2, 1884, Boston, Mass. Graduated, Harvard (1831). Practiced law in Boston.

Wendell Phillips was a vigorous orator, reformer, and abolitionist. He once tore up a copy of the Constitution in public because it did not prohibit the "abomination of human bondage." And he was critical of President Lincoln until the Emancipation Proclamation was issued in 1863. From 1865-70, Phillips was president of the Anti-Slavery Society, keeping it active until the 15th Amendment gave Negroes the right to vote. After the Civil War, he dedicated himself to such reforms as the abolition of capital punishment, protecting the rights of labor, and getting the vote for women.

PHYFE, DUNCAN

Born: 1768, Loch Fannich, near Inverness, Scotland. Died: Aug. 16, 1854, New York City. Brought to U.S. 1783-84.

Duncan Phyfe *(Fife)* was the finest American cabinetmaker of the 1790s and early 1800s. He was apprenticed to an Albany, N.Y., cabinetmaker as a young boy. Later he moved to New York City, where he opened his own joiner's (carpenter's) shop. Eventually he had a work force of more than one hundred artisans. Phyfe's best work was inspired by classic forms, but achieved an individual style of beauty and distinction.

PICKERING, TIMOTHY

Born: July 17, 1745, and Died: Jan. 29, 1829, Salem, Mass. Graduated, Harvard (1763). Adjutant general, Continental army (1777-78). Quartermaster general (1780-83). U.S. Postmaster General (1791-95). Secretary of War (1795). Secretary of State (1795-1800). U.S. senator (1803-11). U.S. congressman (1813-17).

Timothy Pickering, a devoted servant of his country for forty years, was also the sire of a distinguished family. His son John (1777-1846), was a lawyer and student of languages, including those of many American Indian tribes. He compiled the first dictionary of Americanisms *(Vocabulary of Words and Phrases Peculiar to the United States)* (1816). Timothy's grandson, Charles (1805-78), was a noted naturalist. His great grandson, Edward Charles (1846-1919), was an outstanding astronomer and director of the Harvard observatory (1877-1919). He was a specialist in stellar photometry (light measurement) and photography. Edward's brother, William Henry (1858-1938), was also an astronomer. He discovered the ninth satellite of Saturn and predicted and located the planet Pluto (1919).

PIERCE, FRANKLIN

Born: Nov. 23, 1804, Hillsboro, N.H. Died: Oct. 8, 1869, Concord, N.H. Graduated, Bowdoin Coll., Me. (1824). Studied law; admitted to N.H. bar (1827). State legislature (1829-32).

Franklin Pierce

Zebulon Pike (viewing his peak)

U.S. congressman (1833-37). U.S. senator (1837-42). Brigadier general, Mexican War (1845-47).

Franklin Pierce, fourteenth President of the U.S., was named by the Democrats as a compromise candidate. His career had not been distinguished, but he was acceptable to the Southern states because he was generally favorable to slavery. (He believed the Constitution guaranteed it.) He defeated General Winfield Scott in the 1852 election. His administration saw the U.S. extended by the Gadsden Purchase (1853) and the opening of Japan to commerce after Commodore Perry's visit (1854). But it was also marked by national unrest over slavery that later would lead to the Civil War.

PIKE, ZEBULON MONTGOMERY

Born: Jan. 5, 1779, Lamberton, N.J. Died: Apr. 27, 1813, York (now Toronto), Canada.

Captain Pike was leading an expedition (1806-07) to the headwaters of the Arkansas and the Red Rivers as part of a general exploration of the Louisiana Purchase when he discovered the 14,110-foot Colorado peak that bears his name. The son of an army officer, Pike had become a cadet at fifteen, and had already led one expedition up the Mississippi River (1805-06). In 1813, after the War of 1812 began, he was elevated to brigadier general and was killed during a raid against the British in York.

PINCKNEY, CHARLES

Born: Oct. 26, 1757, and Died: Oct. 29, 1824, Charleston, S.C. Served, American Revolution. Continental Congress (1784-87). Constitutional Convention (1787). Governor, S.C. (1789-92, 1796-98, 1806-08). U.S. senator (1798-1801). Minister to Spain (1801-05). U.S. congressman (1819-21).

Charles Pinckney was one of the major contributors to the U.S. Constitution. Although only twenty-nine at the time of the convention (he was the second youngest delegate), he offered a draft constitution so rich in ideas that thirty of its provisions eventually were incorporated in the final document. Together with James Madison and Gouverneur Morris, he was one of the prime movers of the Constitutional Convention.

PINCKNEY, CHARLES COTESWORTH

Born: Feb. 25, 1746, and Died: Aug. 16, 1825, Charleston, S.C. Educated at Oxford, England. Studied military affairs at Royal Academy, Caen, France. Practiced law, Charleston, S.C. (from 1769). Continental army (from 1776), brevetted brigadier general (1783). Constitutional Convention (1787). Federalist candidate for Vice-President (1800) and for President (1804, 1808).

General Pinckney, a cousin of Charles Pinck-

Allan Pinkerton (with Lincoln)

ney, was a distinguished soldier and an ardent Federalist. He fought bravely at Brandywine and Germantown; was captured by the British in 1780 and exchanged in 1782. He was an active delegate to the Constitutional Convention. It was he who urged the idea that no religious test be made as a qualification for government office (Article VI, U.S. Constitution).

PINKERTON, ALLAN

Born: Aug. 25, 1819, Glasgow, Scotland. Died: July 1, 1884, Chicago, Ill. Arrived in U.S. (1842). Deputy sheriff, Kane Co. and Cook Co., Ill. (1848-49).

Allan Pinkerton, head of the first private detective agency in the U.S., won national renown for solving a series of bank and express company robberies. In January, 1861, having learned of a plot to murder Abraham Lincoln, he guarded the President-elect en route to his inauguration. During the Civil War, he was a Union spy and chief of secret-service activities for the Army of the Potomac. After the war he returned to private business, specializing in strikebreaking, industrial spying, and often antiunion activities.

Edgar Allan Poe

POE, EDGAR ALLAN

Born: Jan. 19, 1809, Boston, Mass. Died: Oct. 7, 1849, Baltimore, Md.

Edgar Allan Poe was a writer of wildly imaginative short stories and poetry dealing with the weird, the mysterious, and the horrible. He himself led a restless and disorderly life. Most of his opportunities and successes were cut short by self-destructive actions. He left the U. of Virginia because of gambling debts (1826), was dismissed from West Point for disobedience and neglect of duty (1831), and lost jobs because of uncontrolled drinking. He married, and was devoted to, his fourteen-year-old cousin, Virginia Clemm, but his writing earned only a meager living. The couple existed, happily but in great poverty, until Virginia's death from tuberculosis in 1847.

Among his famous stories are "The Fall of the House of Usher," "The Gold Bug," "The Tell-Tale Heart," and "The Murders in the Rue Morgue," one of the first detective stories. His notable poems include "The Raven," "The Bells," "Annabel Lee," and "Lenore."

POLK, JAMES KNOX

Born: Nov. 2, 1795, Mecklenberg Co., N.C. Died: June 15, 1849, Nashville, Tenn. Graduated, U. of North Carolina (1818). Admitted to N.C. bar (1820). State legislator (1823-25).

James K. Polk

U.S. congressman (1825-39); Speaker of the House (1835-39). Governor of Tenn. (1839-41).

James K. Polk, the eleventh President of the U.S., was an expansionist. During his administration (1845-49), more than 1,000,000 square miles of territory were added to the U.S. He led the nation into the Mexican War (1846-48) through which the present states of Cal., Ariz., N.M., Nev., Utah, and Colo. (west of the Rockies) were acquired. Earlier in 1846 he reached a settlement with Great Britain over the jointly held Oregon Territory. Through this the U.S. gained more land. Polk did not seek re-election.

PORTER, DAVID DIXON

Born: June 8, 1813, Chester, Pa. Died: Feb. 13, 1891, Washington, D.C. Midshipman, U.S. Navy (1829). Served in Mexican and Civil Wars. Superintendent, U.S. Naval Academy (1865-69). Admiral (1870).

During the Civil War, David Porter commanded the mortar fleet (gunboats) that blasted the Confederate forts and enabled Admiral David Farragut to enter the harbor of New Orleans, La., and capture the city (April, 1862). He also engaged the Mississippi River forts at Vicksburg, while the main fleet slipped safely by. In 1863, he co-operated with General Grant in the Siege of Vicksburg.

William Sydney Porter

As superintendent of the Naval Academy, Admiral Porter was responsible for many improvements in curriculum and instruction.

PORTER, WILLIAM SYDNEY (O. Henry)

Born: Sept. 11, 1862, Greensboro, N.C. Died: June 5, 1910, New York City.

William Sydney Porter—more widely known by the pen name O. Henry—was one of America's favorite short-story writers. He had a varied and adventurous background as drug clerk, sheepherder, cowboy, bookkeeper, and banana grower. He spent three years in prison for embezzling funds while a teller in an Austin, Tex., bank. He finally settled in New York City (1902), where he made his living writing for magazines.

His stories are notable for their surprise endings. (In "The Gift of the Magi," the young wife sells her long hair to a wigmaker for money with which to buy her husband a watch fob. He, meanwhile, has sold his watch to buy his wife an expensive comb for her hair.) Collections of his stories appear under such titles as *Cabbages and Kings* (1904), *The Four Million* (1906), and *Waifs and Strays* (1917).

POWELL, JOHN WESLEY

Born: Mar. 24, 1834, Mt. Morris, N.Y. Died: Sept. 23, 1902, Haven, Me. Attended, Illinois, Oberlin, and Wheaton Colls. U.S. Geological Survey (1875-94). Director, Bureau of Ethnology, Smithsonian Institution (1879-1902).

Although he lost his right arm in the Civil War, John Wesley Powell conducted many rigorous expeditions into the West. He was the first white man to journey down the Colorado River (1869) and through the Grand Canyon.

PRENDERGAST, MAURICE BRAZIL

Born: 1859, St. John's, Newfoundland. Died: February 1, 1924, New York City.

Maurice Prendergast was an American painter who worked his way to Europe on a cattle boat in order to study in Paris (1884). Home again, he helped his brother Charles carving picture frames in Winchester, Mass. (1889), then went to New York City, where in 1908 he joined "the Eight." These were artists in rebellion against the formal art then popular in America. Prendergast was an impressionist, whose gay and colorful paintings are now in leading U.S. galleries.

PRESCOTT, WILLIAM HICKLING

Born: May 14, 1796, Salem, Mass. Died: Jan. 28, 1859, Boston, Mass. Graduated, Harvard (1814).

In 1813, an accidental blow from a fellow student nearly blinded William Prescott, but he went on to complete his schooling and become a distinguished historian. He specialized in Spanish history. Much of his research was done by the aid of secretaries who read aloud to him. His best-known works include *History of the Reign of Ferdinand and Isabella the Catholic* (3 vols., 1838), *History of the Conquest of Mexico* (3 vols., 1843), and *History of the Conquest of Peru* (2 vols., 1847). His style and ability to tell a story popularized the reading of history in the U.S.

PULITZER, JOSEPH

Born: Apr. 10, 1847, Mako, Hungary. Died: Oct. 29, 1911, Charleston, S.C. Naturalized citizen (1867). Studied law, admitted to bar (1876). U.S. congressman from N.Y. (1885-86).

Joseph Pulitzer was the publisher of the St. Louis *Post-Dispatch* and New York *Evening World,* founder of the Columbia U. School of

William H. Prescott

Joseph Pulitzer

Journalism, and donor of the Pulitzer prizes. An immigrant boy who came to the U.S. during the Civil War, he served in the Union army and became a journalist at the war's end. He formed the *Post-Dispatch* (1878), bought the *World* (1883), started the *Evening World* (1887). His papers had high standards, introduced many innovations, and were the training ground for many skillful writers and reporters.

The Columbia School of Journalism was founded in 1903. The Pulitzer prizes are awarded annually for excellence in journalism, literature, drama, and music.

PULLMAN, GEORGE MORTIMER

Born: Mar. 31, 1831, Brocton, N.Y. Died: Oct. 19, 1897, Chicago, Ill.

A former shopkeeper and cabinetmaker, George Pullman designed and invented the first railroad sleeping cars for the Chicago and Alton R.R. (1858-59). He devised such improvements as the folding upper berth (1864), the restaurant car (1867), the chair car (1875), and the vestibule car (1887). He founded the Pullman Palace Car Co. in 1867 for their manufacture.

George M. Pullman

I. I. Rabi

R

RABI, ISIDOR ISAAC

Born: July 29, 1898, Rymanow, Austria. Brought to U.S. as an infant. Graduated, Cornell (1919); Columbia, Ph.D. (1927). Postgraduate study in Munich, Hamburg, and Leipzig, Germany; Copenhagen, Denmark, and Zurich, Switzerland. Instructor of physics, Columbia (1929-37); became full professor (1937).

Isidor Rabi (*Rob*-ee) is noted for his research in nuclear physics, magnetism, and molecular structures. During World War II, he engaged in radar research at Massachusetts Institute of Technology and acted as consultant during the development of the first A-bomb.

Dr. Rabi won the Nobel prize in physics (1944), and was twice a presiding officer at the International Conference on Peaceful Uses of Atomic Energy, held at Geneva, Switzerland (1955, 1958).

Edmund Randolph

RANDOLPH, EDMUND

Born: Aug. 10, 1753, near Williamsburg, Va. Died: Sept. 12, 1813, Clarke Co., Va. Attended William and Mary. Studied law privately. Aide-de-camp to George Washington (1775-76). Attorney general, Va. (1776). Member, Continental Congress (1779-82). Governor, Va. (1786-88). Constitutional Convention (1787).

Edmund Randolph became the first Attorney General of the U.S. (1789-94)—an office created by the newly adopted Constitution, which he had played a major role in formulating. (He had, nonetheless, refused to sign it, despite the fact that the final document greatly resembled his own plan for the new government [the Virginia plan].)

In 1794, President George Washington named him Secretary of State, but political differences between the two forced Randolph's resignation (1795).

Returning to Richmond, he resumed the practice of law and was senior counsel for Aaron Burr during the latter's treason trial.

RAYBURN, SAMUEL TALIAFERRO

Born: Jan. 6, 1882, Roane Co., Tenn. Died: Nov. 16, 1961, Bonham, Tex. Graduated, East Texas Normal School (1904). Member, Tex. legislature (1907-12). U.S. congressman (1913-61); Speaker of the House (1940-46, 1949-61).

Sam Rayburn—cordially known as Mister Sam—served in the U.S. House of Representatives for nearly forty-nine years, one of the longest congressional terms in the nation's history. He also was Speaker of the House for seventeen years, more than twice as long as the previous record holder, Henry Clay.

REDFIELD, WILLIAM C.

Born: Mar. 25, 1789, Middletown, Conn. Died: Feb. 12, 1857, New York City.

William Redfield, a saddler and harness maker, was also a pioneer meteorologist (student of the atmosphere). He proved that violent gales are whirlwinds and that the speed of their rotation is greatest at their center, least at the outer edge. He was a founder and first president of the American Association for the Advancement of Science (1848).

REED, WALTER

Born: Sept. 13, 1851, Belroi, Va. Died: Nov. 22, 1902, Washington, D.C. Graduated, U. of Virginia (1869); Bellevue Hospital Medical School, M.D. (1870). Commissioned first lieutenant, U.S. Army Medical Corps (1875). Professor, bacteriology and microscopy, Army Medical Coll., Washington, D.C. (1893).

In 1900, Dr. Reed was sent to Cuba with Drs. Aristides Agramonte, James Carroll, and Jesse Lazear, for the purpose of studying yellow fever, or "Yellow Jack," and how to combat it. Experiments made by Reed and his colleagues proved that yellow fever was carried by a mosquito, the *Aëdes aegypti*. This knowledge made it possible to eliminate the dread disease in the U.S., Cuba, and Panama.

The Walter Reed General Hospital (Washington, D.C.) is named for him.

Walter Reed

REID, WHITELAW

Born: Oct. 27, 1837, near Xenia, Ohio. Died: Dec. 15, 1912, London, England. Graduated, Miami U., O. (1856). Editor, New York Tribune (1872-1905). Minister to France (1889-92). Member, commission to arrange peace with Spain (1898). U.S. ambassador to Great Britain (1905-12).

Whitelaw Reid was one of the fine reporters of the Civil War. His dispatches to the Cincinnati *Gazette* on the Battle of Gettysburg, Pa., the fall of Richmond, Va., and the funeral of Abraham Lincoln were greatly admired by Horace Greeley, and resulted in Reid's appointment as managing editor of the *Tribune* (1868). Reid acquired the paper after Greeley's death and upheld its reputation as one of the leading journals of its time.

REMINGTON, ELIPHALET

Born: Oct. 27, 1793, and Died: Aug. 12, 1861, Suffield, Conn.

Trained as a blacksmith, Eliphalet Remington probably had no idea that he was on the verge of beginning a new career when he one day forged a very fine rifle barrel for himself. Soon he was making them for others. By 1828, he was able to open a factory at Ilion, N.Y.; in 1845, he bought one at Springfield, Mass. Remington rifles were carried by the U.S. Army in both the Mexican and Civil Wars.

In 1847, he began production of the Remington pistol, and in 1856, he added a line of farm implements to his manufactures.

The firearms produced by his plant are today considered milestones in the history of gunmaking, while some of the manufacturing

Frederic Remington

equipment, designed by him for use in his factory, revolutionized the barrelmaking process.

REMINGTON, FREDERIC

Born: Oct. 4, 1861, Canton, N.Y. Died: Dec. 26, 1909, near Ridgefield, Conn. Attended Yale Art School and Art Students League, New York City.

Renowned as an illustrator, painter, and sculptor, Frederic Remington is particularly noted for his sympathetic and realistic representations of the American Indian and of cowboys and soldiers living on the Western plains. He often accompanied the U.S. Army on frontier campaigns so that he could sketch and paint his subjects on location.

When the Spanish-American War broke out, he went to Cuba. There he did many memorable drawings of that conflict for the Hearst newspapers. In all, he completed over 2,700 paintings, drawings, and illustrations during his lifetime.

An author as well as an artist he wrote: *Pony Tracks* (1895), *Crooked Trails* (1898), *Sundown Leflore* (1899), and *John Ermine of the Yellowstone* (1902).

RENWICK, JAMES

Born: Nov. 3, 1818, and Died: June 23, 1895, New York City. Graduated, Columbia (1836).

James Renwick was one of the famous architects of the 19th century. He designed three of New York City's principal churches: Grace Church (1843-46), his first notable building; St. Bartholomew's, and St. Patrick's Cathedral (1853-79). He also designed the original Smithsonian building and the Corcoran Art Gallery in Washington, D.C., and the original Vassar Coll. building at Poughkeepsie, N.Y.

REVERE, PAUL

Born: Jan. 1, 1735, and Died: May 10, 1818, Boston, Mass.

A staunch patriot and member of the Sons of Liberty, Paul Revere is best remembered for his heroic gallop through the Mass. countryside on the eve of the American Revolution (April 18, 1775). That night he rode out to warn patriot leaders in Lexington that the British were coming to arrest them and awakened colonial Minutemen along the way. The feat has been immortalized by Henry Wadsworth Longfellow's poem, "Paul Revere's Ride."

But Revere had other talents besides. He was a dentist, inventor, master silversmith, and cartoonist, whose political cartoons were generally directed against pro-British elements in the colonies. He was also an able leader and businessman. During the Revolution, he commanded American troops at Castle William (1778-79), near Boston, learned how to make gunpowder and ran a factory at Canton, Mass., to produce it. He designed and printed the first issue of Continental money, and made the state seal of Mass. and the first seal of the united colonies.

It was Revere's foundry which after the war cast the bells, made the cannon, and turned out the bolts, pumps, and copper fittings for the warship, *Old Ironsides*. And in 1808 he invented a method of sheet-copper rolling, which made it possible for him to supply the boilers for Robert Fulton's steamboat (1809).

Paul Revere

RICHARDS, ELLEN HENRIETTA

Born: 1842, Dunstable, Mass. Died: 1911, Boston, Mass. Graduated, Vassar (1870). Assistant chemist, Mass. State Board of Health (1872). Organizer and first president, American Home Economics Association (1908).

Ellen Richards was the first woman student admitted to Massachusetts Institute of Technology. She began the study of chemistry there in 1870, and in 1884 was appointed an instructor in sanitary chemistry, a post she held until her death. After her marriage in 1875, she became interested in simplifying the many housekeeping duties of American women. Her studies and innovations were the starting point of the home-economics movement.

RICHARDSON, HENRY HOBSON

Born: Sept. 29, 1838, St. James parish, La. Died: Apr. 28, 1886, Boston, Mass. Graduated, Harvard (1859). Studied at École des Beaux Arts, Paris.

After establishing himself as an architect in N.Y., Henry Richardson moved to Boston (1878) and gained a wide reputation in the profession. He used materials skillfully, and is noted for his free and extremely original adaptation of the French Romanesque style of architecture.

Among his best works are: New Brattle Square and Trinity Church (Boston), his alterations of the state capitol (Albany, N.Y.), Sever Hall and Austin Hall (Harvard), and the county buildings (Pittsburgh, Pa.).

RICKENBACKER, EDWARD VERNON

Born: Oct. 8, 1890, Columbus, Ohio. President, Eastern Air Lines (from 1938).

Captain Eddie Rickenbacker was one of America's World War I heroes. As commander of the 94th Aero Pursuit Squadron in France, he shot down twenty-six German planes and was awarded the Congressional Medal of Honor. Prior to the war he had been a professional auto racer; after the war he had various jobs in the transportation industry until becoming president of E.A.L. During World War II, while on a mission for the air force, the plane he was traveling in was forced to ditch in the Pacific Ocean. He was adrift for twenty-seven days before being rescued. His book, *Seven Came Through* (1943), is an account of this experience.

RIIS, JACOB AUGUST

Born: May 3, 1849, Ribe, Denmark. Died: May 26, 1914, New York City. To U.S. (1870). Reporter, New York Tribune (1877-88), Evening Sun (1888-99).

Jacob Riis *(Rees)* fought slums. Through articles, lectures, and some of the greatest of early documentary photography, he called public attention to the dreadful living conditions in New York City's tenement neighborhoods. His efforts resulted in better schools, new parks and playgrounds, and improved welfare work. He had a good friend and ally in Theodore Roosevelt, and won other support through his books, such as *How the Other Half Lives* (1890), and *The Making of an American* (1901).

RILEY, JAMES WHITCOMB

Born: Oct. 7, 1849, Greenfield, Ind. Died: July 22, 1916, Indianapolis, Ind.

James Whitcomb Riley

David Rittenhouse

Before becoming a poet, James Whitcomb Riley was a sign painter, entertainer, and newspaperman. He first published poems in the Indianapolis *Journal* under the name of Benjamin F. Johnson of Boone.

Most of his verse is written in dialect and deals humorously and sentimentally with the simple aspects of American life. He is warmly referred to as the "Hoosier Poet," and so beloved was he in his home state, that the legislature (1915) declared his birthday a legal holiday.

His works include: *The Old Swimmin' Hole and 'Leven More Poems* (1883), *Afterwhiles* (1887), *Old Fashioned Roses* (1888), *The Little Orphant Annie Book* (1908), and *When the Frost Is on the Punkin* (1911).

RITTENHOUSE, DAVID

Born: Apr. 8, 1732, Germantown, Pa. Died: June 26, 1796, Philadelphia, Pa. Pa. state treasurer (1777-89). Professor, astronomy, U. of Pennsylvania (1779-82). Director, U.S. Mint, Philadelphia (1792-95).

Although self-educated, David Rittenhouse was both a fine watchmaker and an outstanding astronomer. He built a telescope—believed to be the first in America—to trace the orbit of Venus (1768, 1769). He also improved the methods for focusing telescopic equipment.

ROBINSON, EDWIN ARLINGTON

Born: Dec. 22, 1869, Head Tide, Me. Died: Apr. 6, 1935, New York City. Attended Harvard (1891-93).

A master of blank verse, Edwin Arlington Robinson published his first volume of poetry, *The Torrent and the Night Before* in 1896 at his own expense. (The book was reprinted [1897] as *The Children of the Night*.) Afterward, he lived in poverty in New York City, where he worked on the construction of the city's subway (1904-05). When President Theodore Roosevelt, an admirer of Robinson's work, learned of the young poet's difficulties, he appointed him to the New York customs service (1905-09).

Between 1911-35, Robinson gained fame in both the U.S. and Europe. He was awarded three Pulitzer prizes in poetry for *Collected Poems* (1922), *The Man Who Died Twice* (1925), and *Tristram* (1928).

ROCKEFELLER, JOHN DAVISON

Born: July 8, 1839, Richford, N.Y. Died: May 23, 1937, Ormond Beach, Fla.

More than any other name in American history, the name John D. Rockefeller has become synonymous with great wealth. He was probably the nation's first billionaire. His rise to fame began at the close of the Civil War, when he and his brother, William (1841-1922), set up an oil-refining company, later known as the Standard Oil Co. (1867). Within a few years, under John Rockefeller's guidance, it was an overwhelmingly successful business venture, and Rockefeller was soon merging his oil interests with transportation interests, so that he could ship oil at cheaper rates than his competitors. By the late 1880s, he controlled nine tenths of the oil-refining industry and several subsidiary businesses as well.

John D. Rockefeller

The Rockefeller domination was brought to an end in 1911 by the employment of the Sherman Anti-Trust Act. However, Standard Oil remained a giant in the petroleum field. That same year (1911), Rockefeller retired from active participation in the business in favor of his son, John D., Jr. (1874-1960). In his later years, John, Sr., founded the Rockefeller Institute of Medical Research (1901) and the Rockefeller Foundation (1913). He also gave financial help to the U. of Chicago (1892).

RODGERS, JOHN

Born: 1773. Died: 1838.

John Rodgers was the first of several generations of a family dedicated to service in the U.S. Navy. He ranked captain in 1799, fought the Barbary pirates in the Mediterranean (1802-06), and saw action in the War of 1812. His son, John (1812-82), drew valuable charts and surveys while on naval expeditions to the North Pacific, the Arctic, and the China coast. During the Civil War, he captured a Confederate ironclad. He became a rear admiral (1870) and superintendent of the Naval Observatory in Washington, D.C. (1877-82). A grandson, William Ledyard Rodgers (1860-1944), became a rear admiral by 1924. A great grandson, John (1881-1926), was on North Atlantic submarine duty during World War I.

The original John's brother, George Washington Rodgers (1787-1832), served during the War of 1812. And *his* son, Christopher Raymond Perry Rodgers (1819-92), fought in the Seminole War (1839-42), the Civil War (in one action he and cousin John [1812-82] were on the same ship), and became superintendent of the Naval Academy (1874-78) and commander in chief of the Pacific Squadron (1878-80).

RODGERS, RICHARD

Born: 1902, New York City. Attended Columbia and Institute of Musical Art, N.Y.

Richard Rodgers has been composing a great number of America's favorite songs since 1925. In that year he and his long-time friend and lyricist, Lorenz Hart (1895-1943), collaborated on *The Garrick Gaieties,* the first of a long series of musical hits. Others included: *A Connecticut Yankee* (1927), *On Your Toes* (1936), *Babes in Arms* (1937), *I'd Rather Be Right* (1937), *I Married an Angel* (1938), *The Boys from Syracuse* (1938), *Pal Joey* (1940).

In 1943, Rodgers began a second fruitful partnership, this time with Oscar Hammerstein II. Their *Oklahoma* set new high standards for the musical stage, and was followed by *Carousel* (1945), *South Pacific* (1949), *The King and I* (1952), and *The Sound of Music* (1961), among others.

ROEBLING, JOHN AUGUSTUS

Born: June 12, 1806, Mühlhausen, Germany. Died: July 22, 1869, Brooklyn, N.Y. Graduated, Royal Polytechnic Institute, Berlin, Germany (1826). U.S. citizen (1837).

John A. Roebling came to the U.S. in 1831, and after working at various types of engineering jobs, established a factory to manufacture the first wire rope made in America (1841).

However, he is chiefly remembered for his work on suspension bridges. His first over the Monongahela River at Pittsburgh, Pa., was completed in 1846. His others include the railroad span at Niagara Falls (1851-55).

In 1857, he suggested the possibility of a bridge across the East River to link Brooklyn and Manhattan. The idea was approved (1869), and as construction on the world-famous Brooklyn Bridge was about to get underway, Roebling suffered an injury at the bridge site (June 28, 1869), developed tetanus, and died days later.

The work was completed by his son, Washington Augustus Roebling (1837-1926), and the bridge now stands as a monument to its originator.

Washington A. Roebling

Will Rogers

ROGERS, WILL (William Penn Adair)

Born: Nov. 4, 1879, Oologah, Indian Territory (now Claremore, Okla.). Died: Aug. 15, 1935, near Point Barrow, Alaska.

Humorist, actor, and writer, Will Rogers was one of the best-loved Americans of all time. He started out as a cowboy in his native Okla., where he learned to handle a lasso so well that he worked it into a vaudeville act. It was the humorous chitchat, however, which he later added to his lasso feats that made him so successful.

His stage career began in 1905, when he first appeared at Hammerstein's Roof Garden. After nine years on the vaudeville circuits, Rogers became an overnight sensation in the "Ziegfeld Follies" (1914).

During his lifetime, he appeared in numerous motion pictures. He also entertained Americans with a syndicated newspaper column (1926-35), and a radio show, in which he made witty comments on current events.

Rogers was killed when a plane piloted by his friend, world-famous aviator Wiley Post (1900-35), crashed with the two men aboard during a flight over Alaska.

Eleanor Roosevelt

Franklin D. Roosevelt

ROOSEVELT, ANNA ELEANOR

Born: Oct. 11, 1884, and Died: Nov. 7, 1962, New York City. Chairwoman, Commission on Human Rights (Economic and Social Council, United Nations).

Eleanor Roosevelt, who once described herself as "painfully shy," nevertheless became one of the nation's most prominent figures and the center of much public attention in her later years.

Throughout her life, she was an able and vigorous worker for the improved living conditions of her fellow man. Her marriage (1905) to a distant cousin, Franklin Delano Roosevelt, provided her with greater opportunity to serve her country and mankind.

During the early years of her husband's political career, she remained in the background, but when F.D.R. was stricken with poliomyelitis (1920) and left partially paralyzed, she began to take a more active role. She assisted him greatly during two successful N.Y. gubernatorial campaigns (1928, 1930) and during four terms as President (1933-45). She worked with him to obtain much-needed educational and social reforms in the lean years of the 1930s, and when World War II broke out, served as assistant director of Civilian Defense. She also made visits to England (1942), the Southwest Pacific (1943), and the Caribbean (1944).

After her husband's death (April, 1945), she was appointed U.S. delegate to the U.N. General Assembly (1945, 1949-52), where she distinguished herself in the field of foreign diplomacy and continued her crusade for humanitarian causes.

She is the author of several books—the most successful, *This I Remember* (1949) and *On My Own* (1958)—and for many years wrote a daily newspaper column, "My Day."

ROOSEVELT, FRANKLIN DELANO

Born: Jan. 30, 1882, Hyde Park, N.Y. Died: Apr. 12, 1945, Warm Springs, Ga. Graduated, Harvard (1904) and Columbia Law School (1907). Practiced law in New York City. N.Y. state senator (1911-13). Assistant Secretary of the Navy (1913-20). Governor, N.Y. (1929-33).

Franklin Delano Roosevelt, thirty-first President of the U.S., was the first man to be elected for four consecutive terms. He became President by defeating Herbert Hoover in 1932, at the depth of the great depression. Although the economy was faltering and millions of people were out of work, F.D.R. inspired Americans by promising a new deal. "The only thing we have to fear," he said in his inaugural address, "is fear itself."

Throughout his first term, Roosevelt pushed a bold program of economic and social legislation. He defeated Governor Alfred M. Landon of Kan. in 1936 to win a second term.

By 1940, World War II had begun in Europe and was threatening the U.S. The nation had a strong tradition that no President should serve more than two terms, but F.D.R.'s experience in office made him a logical candidate. He defeated Wendell L. Willkie, of Ind. In 1944, the U.S. was itself engaged in World War II, and Roosevelt was an easy winner over Thomas E. Dewey, the racket-busting attorney from N.Y.

Roosevelt supported Great Britain against Nazi Germany after the fall of France (1940), and mobilized a total war effort after Japan bombed Pearl Harbor (December 7, 1941—described by Roosevelt as "a date which will live in infamy").

He led the nation through the peril of the war years, but died just as victory over Germany and Japan was in sight. Death came only three months after the start of his fourth term, while he was visiting Warm Springs, Ga. This was where he had been treated in the 1920s, while waging a courageous personal fight against the crippling effects of polio. He set up a foundation for other polio victims at Warm Springs, in appreciation for his triumph over the disease, and always enjoyed visiting there.

Vice-President Harry S. Truman assumed the presidency on his death.

ROOSEVELT, THEODORE

Born: Oct. 27, 1858, New York City. Died: Jan. 6, 1919, Oyster Bay, N.Y. Graduated, Harvard (1880). N.Y. legislature (1882-84). Member, U.S. Civil Service Commission (1889-95). Police commissioner, New York City (1895-97). Assistant Secretary of the Navy (1897-98).

Theodore Roosevelt, twenty-fifth President of the U.S., was handicapped as a boy by weak eyesight and a frail body. He had a determined spirit, however, and afterward lived a vigorous, energetic life.

During the Spanish-American War, Roosevelt organized a volunteer cavalry unit known as the Rough Riders. Its colorful and successful charge up San Juan Hill in Cuba won fame for the unit and national prominence for Colonel "Teddy" Roosevelt. He was elected gov-

Theodore Roosevelt

ernor of N.Y. (1898) and became President William McKinley's running mate (1900). When McKinley was assassinated the following year, Teddy became President. He was elected to the office in 1904, defeating Democrat Alton B. Parker (1852-1926).

The Roosevelt administration was an active one. Antitrust laws were passed to break up big business combines. Natural resources were protected by conservation laws. A pure food and drug law and a law providing for government inspection of meat were passed.

Between 1904 and 1914, the Panama Canal was built (after Teddy used power politics to get rights to the Canal Zone). In 1905, he mediated the Russo-Japanese War, an effort for which he was awarded the Nobel peace prize (1906). He believed in national military preparedness and said it was wisest to "Speak softly and carry a big stick; you will go far."

After leaving the White House, Roosevelt made an extended trip abroad and hunted wild game in Africa. In 1912, disappointed in his hand-picked successor, President Taft, he tried—and failed—to get the Republican nomination again. He ran as the nominee of the Progressive ("Bull Moose") party, but finished third behind Woodrow Wilson, the winner, and the Republican candidate, Taft.

ROOT, ELIHU

Born: Feb. 15, 1845, Clinton, N.Y. Died: Feb. 7, 1937, New York City. Graduated, Hamilton Coll., N.Y. (1865); New York U. Law School (1867). Practiced law in New York City. U.S. senator (1909-15). Member Permanent Court of Arbitration, The Hague, Holland (1910).

Twice Secretary of War (1899-1904), under Presidents McKinley and Theodore Roosevelt, and once Secretary of State (1905-09), under

Elihu Root

T.R., Elihu Root did much to formulate American foreign policy at the turn of the century. He drew up a constitution for the Philippines (then a U.S. possession), improved U.S. relations with South America, and in 1908 negotiated an "open-door agreement" with Japan, leading to freer trade relations.

From 1910-25, Root headed the Carnegie Endowment for International Peace, and was awarded a Nobel peace prize for his vigorous work (1912).

After World War I, he led a special diplomatic mission to Russia, advocated U.S. participation in the League of Nations, and served as a member of the committee of jurists at The Hague (1920-21), which set up the Permanent Court of International Justice.

The author of several books on international diplomacy, Root's best known work is *Russia and the United States* (1917).

ROOT, GEORGE FREDERICK

Born: Aug. 30, 1820, Sheffield, Mass. Died: Aug. 6, 1895, Bailey's Island, Me.

A musician, composer, and music publisher, George Root wrote words and music for many famous Civil War tunes, among them: "Tramp, Tramp, Tramp, the Boys are Marching," "The Battle Cry of Freedom," and "Just Before the Battle, Mother."

ROSENWALD, JULIUS

Born: Aug. 12, 1862, Springfield, Ill. Died: Jan. 6, 1932, Chicago, Ill.

Julius Rosenwald was one of the leading developers of the mail-order business in the U.S. He perfected this method of merchandising while acting as vice-president and treasurer (1895-1910) and as president (1910-25) of Sears, Roebuck and Co.

More important, however, he used the millions his success in the business world brought him to create the Julius Rosenwald Fund (1917) for the "well-being of mankind." He did much to aid the education and welfare of American Negroes and to alleviate injustices to Jewish peoples in the Near East. He also founded the Museum of Science and Industry, Chicago, Ill. (1929).

ROSS, BETSY

Born: 1752, and Died: Jan. 30, 1836, Philadelphia, Pa.

Elizabeth Griscom Ross is known to have

Julius Rosenwald

Betsy Ross

made flags during the Revolution, but historians are now generally agreed that she did not design or make the first Stars and Stripes at George Washington's request. (The Continental Congress voted that the Stars and Stripes should be the country's national emblem on June 14, 1777.)

ROSS, JOHN

Born: Oct. 30, 1790, near Lookout Mountain, Tenn. Died: Aug. 1, 1866, Washington, D.C.

John Ross was a leader of the Cherokee Indians. He was the son of a Scottish father and a part-Cherokee mother; his Indian name was Koowesкoowe. He served with Andrew Jackson against the Creek Indians in 1812. And as chief of the Eastern Cherokee Nation (1828-39), he struggled to keep the tribal lands from being overrun by white settlers. Eventually he was forced to lead the Cherokees westward to treaty lands in Okla. There he was chief of the United Cherokee Nation (1839-66).

ROSS, NELLIE TAYLOE

Born: 1880, St. Joseph, Mo.

Nellie Tayloe Ross was the first woman to become the governor of a state and the director of the U.S. Mint. She was elected governor of Wyo. (1925-27) to finish the incompleted term of her husband, William Bradford Ross, who had died. She was appointed director of the Mint by President Franklin Roosevelt in 1933 and served for twenty years.

ROWLAND, HENRY AUGUSTUS

Born: Nov. 27, 1848, Honesdale, Pa. Died: Apr. 16, 1901, Baltimore, Md. Graduated, Rensselaer Polytechnic Institute, N.Y. (1870). Taught physics at Rensselaer Polytechnic Institute (1872-75). First professor of physics, newly established Johns Hopkins U. (1876-1901). Consultant on installation of equipment at Niagara Falls power plant.

A pioneer in the fields of optics and electricity, and the author of many papers on these subjects, Henry Rowland is especially noted for his work on the solar spectrum, for his many contributions to the modern theory of electrons, and for his research into the theory of alternating currents. In addition, his studies in the field of magnetism were essential to the development of transformers and dynamos.

ROYCE, JOSIAH

Born: Nov. 20, 1855, Grass Valley, Cal. Died: Sept. 14, 1916, Cambridge, Mass. Graduated, U. of California (1875); Johns Hopkins, Ph.D. (1878). Taught English, U. of California (1878-82). Professor, philosophy, Harvard (1882-1916).

An outstanding American philosopher, and a student of history and science as well, Josiah Royce developed a school of thought based, in general, on the concept that a purposeful life necessitated the moral independence of the individual. Much of Royce's writings is idealistic in content. His textbooks on philosophy include: *Studies in Good and Evil* (1898), *The World and the Individual* (2 vols., 1900-01), *The Philosophy of Loyalty* (1908), and *The Hope of the Great Community* (1916).

Josiah Royce

Benjamin Rush

RUSH, BENJAMIN

Born: Dec. 24, 1745, Byberry (now Philadelphia), Pa. Died: Apr. 19, 1813, Philadelphia, Pa. Graduated, Coll. of New Jersey (Princeton) (1760); U. of Edinburgh, Scotland, M.D. (1768). First professor of chemistry in colonies, Coll. and Academy of Philadelphia (1769-91). Member, Continental Congress (1776-77). Professor, medicine and clinical practice, U. of Pennsylvania (1792-1813). Treasurer, U.S. Mint, Philadelphia (1799). Founder, first American antislavery society.

Dr. Benjamin Rush was a signer of the Declaration of Independence (1776) and during the Revolution served as surgeon general of the Continental army (1777-78). Afterward, he established the first free dispensary in the U.S. (1786) at Philadelphia and made important contributions to the development of medicine through his teachings and writings.

RUSSELL, WILLIAM HEPBURN

Born: Jan. 31, 1812, Burlington, Vt. Died: Sept. 10, 1872, Palmyra, Mo.

As president of the Central Overland California and Pike's Peak Express Co., William Hepburn Russell became important for his work in developing Western stagecoach lines. He also organized the Pony Express (1860), which carried the mail between St. Joseph, Mo., and Sacramento, Cal., in the then unheard of time of ten days.

RUTLEDGE, JOHN

Born: Sept., 1739, and Died: July 18, 1800, Charleston, S.C. Attorney general, S.C. (1764-65). Member, Continental Congress, (1774-76, 1782-83). President, S.C. (1776-78); governor (1779-82). Delegate, Constitutional Convention (1787). Associate justice, U.S. Supreme Court (1789-91).

John Rutledge began a long career of statesmanship when he joined the S.C. provincial assembly at the age of twenty-three. He served S.C. in a variety of posts and was an active patriot during the American Revolution. He contributed greatly to the development of the U.S. Constitution and helped get it accepted in S.C. as a member of the state ratification convention (1780). He was one of the first appointees to the Supreme Court.

RYDER, ALBERT PINKHAM

Born: Mar. 19, 1847, New Bedford, Mass. Died: Mar. 28, 1917, Elmhurst, N.Y.

Albert Pinkham Ryder

Albert Ryder was a largely self-taught artist who lived as a recluse, indifferent to comfort or success and dedicated only to his painting. Most of his work was far ahead of its time in technique and style. His pictures are in many major museum collections. Among the best known are *Death on a Pale Horse, Toilers of the Sea, The Flying Dutchman.*

S

SACAGAWEA

This remarkable Indian woman was the guide and interpreter for the Lewis and Clark expedition (1804-06) when it reached the territory of the upper Missouri River. Little is known of her. She was a member of a Western tribe, probably the Shoshone. She had been captured and eventually traded to—and married by—Toussaint Charbonneau, the Canadian trapper who was the expedition's official interpreter. In the remote wilderness of the West, Sacagawea (Sacka-ja-*wee*-a) proved a skillful and tireless guide, and a highly respected interpreter.

SAINT-GAUDENS, AUGUSTUS

Born: Mar. 1, 1848, Dublin, Ireland. Died: Aug. 3, 1907, Cornish, N.H. Studied at Cooper Union. Attended the National Academy of Design and École des Beaux Arts in Paris.

Even as a young apprentice to a New York cameo cutter, Augustus Saint-Gaudens (Sant-*Gaw*-dnz) showed a talent for sculpture. His first success was a likeness of Hiawatha (1871). Others include his statue of Lincoln (1887), in Lincoln Park, Chicago, Ill.; of Admiral Farragut (1881) in Madison Square, N.Y., and the equestrian statue of General William T. Sherman (1903) at the entrance to New York City's Central Park. Perhaps his most famous work is the commanding figure of Deacon Chapin, often called *The Puritan* (1885), at Springfield, Mass.

SALK, JONAS

Born: Oct. 28, 1914, New York City. Graduated, City Coll. of New York (1934); New York Coll. of Medicine, M.D. (1939). Studied, U. of Pittsburgh School of Medicine. Virus research laboratory director (1947).

With funds made available by the National Foundation for Infantile Paralysis, Salk began work (1951) on a vaccine to prevent polio. Two years later he announced a trial vaccine. It was tested in a mass trial, and in 1954 pronounced safe and eighty to ninety per cent effective. Among the many honors he received for his life-saving discovery was the Medal for Distinguished Civilian Achievement, awarded (1955) by Congress.

SALOMON, HAYM

Born: 1740, Leszno, Poland. Died: Jan. 6, 1785, Philadelphia, Pa.

Haym Salomon helped finance the American Revolution. An immigrant who had established a prosperous brokerage in Philadephia, he joined the patriot cause and helped Robert Morris to arrange for the foreign and domestic loans necessary to carry on the war. He pledged his own fortune to strengthen American credit and gave funds totaling some $650,000, an

Augustus Saint-Gaudens

enormous sum in the 18th century. During the British occupation of New York City (1776), he was twice arrested, once as a spy and once for urging Hessian soldiers to desert.

SANDBURG, CARL

Born: Jan. 6, 1878, Galesburg, Ill. Attended Lombard Coll. (now Knox Coll.), O.

Carl Sandburg is a poet, biographer, folk singer, and historian. His *Chicago Poems,* like most of his poetry in free verse, established him (1916) as a grass-roots American poet. His *Complete Poems* won a Pulitzer poetry prize in 1951. An outstanding Lincoln scholar, Sandburg wrote a great biography of the martyred President: *The Prairie Years* (1926) and *The War Years* (1939), for which he won the Pulitzer prize in history (1940). He is also a collector of folk ballads and edited *The American Songbag* (1927), wrote *Rootabaga Stories* (1922) for children, and an autobiography, *Always the Young Strangers* (1953).

SARGENT, JOHN SINGER

Born: 1856, Florence, Italy. Died: Apr. 14, 1925, London, England.

John Singer Sargent was born and educated abroad, and while still in his twenties won an international reputation as a portrait painter. He made frequent trips to the U.S., but spent most of his life in London, portraying members of English and American society.

He is also known for a series of murals, *The History of Religion,* done between 1890 and 1916 for the Boston (Mass.) Public Library, and for some impressionistic water colors of Venice and the Tyrol, painted in the last decade of his life.

SCHIRRA, WALTER MARTY, JR.

(All astronauts listed under CARPENTER, MALCOLM SCOTT, Vol. 11.)

SCHOOLCRAFT, HENRY ROWE

Born: Mar. 28, 1793, near Albany, N.Y. Died: Dec. 10, 1864, Washington, D.C.

While Indian agent for the Great Lakes region, Henry Schoolcraft discovered the source of the Mississippi River (1832) in Lake Itsaca, Minn. He also journeyed down the Ohio River and surveyed northern Mich. and the Upper Great Lakes area. He learned the Ojibway language from his half-Indian wife and made many valuable studies of the Ojibway tribe.

Jonas Salk

Walter M. Schirra, Jr.

SCHURZ, CARL

Born: Mar. 2, 1829, Cologne, Germany. Died: May 14, 1906, New York City. U.S. minister to Spain (1861). U.S. senator from Mo. (1869-75). Secretary of the Interior (1877-81). Editor, New York Evening Post (1881-83). Editorial writer, Harper's Weekly (1892-98).

Carl Schurz *(Shirts)* was a politician. He fled Germany (1852) after his arrest for taking part in a political uprising, came to the U.S., and became an active Republican. He campaigned for Lincoln in 1860 and was rewarded with a diplomatic post in Spain. He resigned to fight in the Civil War, was a major general of volunteers at Chancellorsville, Va., and Gettysburg, Pa. Afterward, as President Hayes' Secretary of the Interior, he carried out widespread reforms in the treatment of the Indians.

Carl Schurz

Winfield Scott

SCOTT, WINFIELD

Born: June 13, 1786, near Petersburg, Va. Died: May 29, 1866, West Point, N.Y. Joined army (1808). Commanding general, U.S. Army (1841-61).

Winfield Scott was one of the great soldiers of American history. His troops nicknamed him "Old Fuss and Feathers" because of his vanity and his elaborate uniforms, but he was a daring strategist, a bold fighter, and considerate of his men. He performed so gallantly in the War of 1812 that he was promoted from captain to major general and became a national hero.

During the Mexican War, he shared honors with Zachary Taylor. Scott took Vera Cruz (with navy co-operation) in early 1847, stormed Chapultepec in September, and entered Mexico City shortly thereafter.

He also had a talent for diplomacy and settled several boundary disputes and many Indian problems.

Despite his Va. background, he remained loyal to the Union in the Civil War and commanded the Union armies in the early months of the conflict. In November, 1861, he was replaced by George McClellan because of old age and ill health. President Lincoln and his entire cabinet paid a call on the old general in tribute to his lifetime of service to the nation.

SEABORG, GLENN THEODORE

Born: Apr. 19, 1912, Ishpeming, Mich. Graduated, U. of California (1934); professor of chemistry (1945-58); chancellor (1958-61). Chairman of the Atomic Energy Commission (from 1961).

A co-winner of the 1951 Nobel prize in chemistry with Dr. E. M. McMillan for discovering plutonium, which supplied a triggering substance for the atom bomb, Glenn Seaborg has long been engaged in chemical research. He worked on the "Manhattan Project" (A-bomb) from 1942-46, and in the course of his researches discovered four elements in addition to plutonium: americum (95), curium (96), berkelium (97), and californium (98).

Glenn Seaborg

SEE, THOMAS JEFFERSON JACKSON

Born: Feb. 19, 1866, near Montgomery City, Mo. Graduated, U. of Missouri (1889). Organized astronomy department, U. of Chicago (1893-96). Astronomer, Lowell Observatory, Flagstaff, Ariz. (1896-98). Professor of mathematics, U. S. Navy (from 1899). Director, Naval Observatory, Mare Island, Cal. (from 1903).

Thomas See was an outstanding astronomer who surveyed the stars of the southern skies, studying and mapping some 200,000 fixed stars and discovering and measuring some 600 new "double stars." He established the astronomy department of the new U. of Chicago and was among the scientists who set up the famed Yerkes Observatory at Williams Bay, Wis.

SEQUOYAH

Born: 1770, Loudon Co., Tenn. Died: 1843, near San Fernandino, Mexico.

Sequoyah (See-*kwoy*-a), whose English name was George Guess, was the son of a Cherokee Indian girl and a white trader. While working in the Cherokee country in Ga., Sequoyah became aware of the need for a system of writing the language of his people and prepared to devise one. By borrowing some letters from the English-language alphabet and creating new ones from sounds peculiar to the Cherokee tongue, he worked out a table of eighty-six characters (about 1821). It was an extremely simple system and he proved it a practical one during a visit to Ark. (1822). There he taught thousands of Cherokee Indians to read and write. His "alphabet" not only helped to unite the Cherokee tribe, but made it possible to print books in Cherokee and to establish a Cherokee newspaper in Okla., in 1828.

The Sequoia tree was named in his honor.

Sequoyah

SEWARD, WILLIAM HENRY

Born: May 16, 1801, Florida, N.Y. Died: Oct. 10, 1872, Auburn, N.Y. Graduated, Union Coll. (1820). Admitted to N.Y. bar (1822); began practice, Auburn, N.Y. (1823). State senator (1830-34). Governor of N.Y. (1839-43). U.S. senator (1849-61).

William Henry Seward was an open critic of slavery and the friend of the foreign-born, especially newly arrived immigrants, whom he helped in many ways. A prominent Republican senator in the difficult years before the Civil War, he twice sought to run as his party's presidential candidate (1856, 1860), but lost to John Charles Frémont and Abraham Lincoln.

He served skillfully as Secretary of State for both Lincoln and Johnson. In 1867, he bought Alaska from Russia for $7,200,000—a bargain his critics could not appreciate and mocked as "Seward's folly."

SHEPARD, ALAN BARTLETT, JR.

(All astronauts listed under CARPENTER, MALCOLM SCOTT, Vol. 11.)

Alan B. Shepard, Jr.

Phil Sheridan

SHERIDAN, PHILIP HENRY

Born: Mar. 6, 1831, Albany, N.Y. Died: Aug. 5, 1888. Graduated, West Point (1853). Commanding general, U.S. Army (1883). Promoted to general (1888).

"Little Phil" Sheridan was a daring and ruthless cavalry officer. Appointed commander of the Army of the Potomac's cavalry by General Grant in April, 1864, he immediately launched a raid beyond the Wilderness, behind Lee's lines. He disrupted communications, destroyed supplies, and gave the Confederate cavalryman, J.E.B. Stuart, a beating besides. In August, 1864, he cleared Jubal Early's raiders out of the Shenandoah Valley. In April, 1865, his vigorous pursuit of Lee's retreating army enabled him to cut the Confederates off at Appomattox Court House.

SHERMAN, ROGER

Born: Apr. 19, 1721, Newton, Mass. Died: July 23, 1793, New Haven, Conn. Member, Continental Congress (1774-81, 1783-84). Delegate,

Roger Sherman

Constitutional Convention (1787). U.S. congressman (1789-91). U.S. senator (1791-93).

Roger Sherman is the only man to have signed the four major documents of American history. A Conn. judge and legislator, he was a strong patriot who helped draw up the Articles of Association (1774), the Declaration of Independence (1776), the Articles of Confederation (1778), and the Constitution (1787).

SHERMAN, WILLIAM TECUMSEH

Born: Feb. 8, 1820, Lancaster, O. Died: Feb. 14, 1891, New York City. Graduated, West Point (1840). Served in the Mexican War (1846-47). Commander in chief, U.S. Army (1869-84).

William Tecumseh Sherman resigned from the U.S. Army in 1853 to enter the banking business in San Francisco, Cal. His bank failed (1855), and he took a post as superintendent of the Louisiana Military Academy, Alexandria, La. Back in the army at the outbreak of the Civil War, Sherman commanded a brigade at First Bull Run, Va. (1861) and a division at Shiloh, Tenn. (1862), and took an important part in capturing Vicksburg, Miss. (1863). When Grant became commander in chief of the Union armies, Sherman replaced his old friend as commander of the Mississippi Military District (March, 1864). In May, he marched out of Chattanooga, Tenn., and invaded Ga., capturing Atlanta in September, 1864. With 62,000 men, he then made his famous "March to the Sea," which ended in Savannah, Ga., in December. Leaving Savannah (1865), he marched through the Carolinas and forced the surrender of General Joseph E. Johnston at Durham, N.C.

Prominently mentioned as a Republican presidential candidate (1884), Sherman declared: "If nominated I will not run, if elected I will not serve." He is also noted for the statement, "War is hell!"

SHERWOOD, ROBERT EMMETT

Born: Apr. 4, 1896, New Rochelle, N.Y. Died: Nov. 14, 1955, New York City. Graduated, Harvard (1918). Canadian Expeditionary Force, (1917-19). Staff member, Life (1920-24); editor (1924-28).

Robert E. Sherwood was a major American playwright. His first success was *The Road to Rome* (1927); other plays included *Waterloo Bridge* (1930), *Reunion in Vienna* (1931), *The Petrified Forest* (1934), and three Pulitzer-prize-winning plays: *Idiot's Delight* (1936), *Abe Lincoln in Illinois* (1938), and *There Shall Be No Night* (1940).

During World War II, Sherwood was director of overseas operations of the Office of War Information. He was also one of President Franklin Roosevelt's principal speech writers. In 1948, he wrote *Roosevelt and Hopkins*, which won a Pulitzer prize for biography.

SINCLAIR, UPTON BEALL

Born: Sept. 20, 1878, Baltimore, Md. Graduated, Coll. of the City of New York (1897).

Upton Sinclair has written more than seventy books, none more famous than his first, *The Jungle* (1906). This was an exposé of unsanitary conditions in the meat-packing industry and helped bring about the Federal Pure Food and Drug law. At this time, Sinclair was numbered among "the muckrakers," a group of crusading journalists that was bringing ugly economic and social conditions to public attention in leading magazines.

Sinclair carried his crusading into politics in 1934, when he ran as the Democratic candidate for governor of Cal. on a platform which promised to "end poverty in California," and so became known as the "EPIC" movement. He was an unsuccessful candidate, however.

Among his other books are: *King Coal* (1917), *The Brass Check* (1919), and *Dragon's Teeth* (1942), a Pulitzer prize winner (1943).

SLATER, SAMUEL

Born: June 9, 1768, Derbyshire, England. Died: Apr. 23, 1835, Webster, Mass.

Samuel Slater broke Britain's monopoly on cotton-milling machinery. In the 18th century, English law forbade the export of machinery models or plans and the emigration of textile workers. Slater, a plant superviser thoroughly familiar with the Arkwright cotton-spinning machinery, left England in disguise, and came to the U.S. (1789). Through a remarkable feat of memory, he was able to reproduce the cotton-manufacturing machinery and thus begin the U.S. cotton industry (1790).

SLAYTON, DONALD KENT

(All astronauts listed under CARPENTER, MALCOLM SCOTT, Vol. 11.)

SLOAN, JOHN

Born: Aug. 2, 1871, Lock Haven, Pa. Died: Sept. 8, 1951, Hanover, N.H. Instructor, Art Students League, New York City (1914-24), and president (1930-51).

John Sloan, now regarded as a distinguished American painter, was founder (1908) and leader of "the Eight," a group of young artists protesting the airless formality of American art. Their critics called them the "Ash Can School" because of their interest in everyday subjects, bold colors, and inventive new techniques. Sloan and his group were responsible for the famous Armory Show in New York City (1913), introducing modern European artists, such as Picasso and Matisse, to a shocked U.S. Sloan's own paintings include *Hotel Lafayette, McSorley's Bar,* and *Wake of the Ferry.*

Al Smith

SMITH, ALFRED EMANUEL

Born: Oct. 30, 1873, and Died: Oct. 5, 1944, New York City. N.Y. state legislature (1903-15). N.Y. county sheriff (1915-17). President, Board of Aldermen, N.Y. (1917). Elected governor, N.Y. (1918, 1922, 1924, 1926).

Al Smith, the "Happy Warrior," was one of N.Y. state's more progressive governors. During his four terms, much social legislation (minimum wage for women, health insurance for industrial workers, state government reorganization) was passed. By 1928, he was the nation's outstanding Democrat, and was nominated for the presidency. He was also a Roman Catholic and a "wet" (against the prohibition of liquor). He was defeated by the Republican candidate, Herbert Hoover.

SMITH, ERMINNIE ADELLE PLATT

Born: Apr. 26, 1836, Marcellus, N.Y. Died: June 9, 1886, Jersey City, N.J.

Erminnie Smith was engaged (1878) by the Smithsonian Institution to study the languages and customs of the Iroquois Indians. To learn the Indian way of life more intimately, she became a member of the Tuscarora tribe. She produced one of the first Iroquois-English dictionaries.

SMITH, THEOBALD

Born: July 31, 1859, Albany, N.Y. Died: Dec. 10, 1934, New York City. Graduated, Cornell (1881) and Albany Medical Coll. (1883). Professor, Harvard (1896-1915). A director, Rockefeller Institute for Medicine (1915-29); president (1933-34).

Theobald Smith was an immunologist (scientist specializing in developing the body's resistance to disease). In 1886 he demonstrated an immunizing method for cholera. In 1889 he discovered the organism that caused Texas fever in cattle, and proved it was passed on by the cattle tick. In 1898 he described the differences between the human and bovine tuberculosis bacilli.

SOUSA, JOHN PHILIP

Born: Nov. 6, 1854, Washington, D.C. Died: March 6, 1932, Reading, Pa.

John Philip Sousa, the "March King," was made director of the U.S. Marine band (1880). Twelve years later, he organized Sousa's Band and gave concerts all over the U.S. and throughout Europe, where King Edward VII of England decorated him with the Victorian Order. Among the famous marches he composed are: "Semper Fidelis" (1888), "Stars and Stripes Forever" (1897), "Washington Post March" (1889), and "Liberty Bell" (1893).

SPAATZ, CARL ANDREW

Born: June 28, 1891, Boyertown, Pa. Graduated, West Point (1914). Commander, U.S. Air

John Philip Sousa

Carl A. Spaatz

Forces in Europe (1942). Commanding general (1946-47) and chief of staff (1947-48), U.S. Air Forces.

Carl "Tooey" Spaatz *(Spots)* commanded the American bomber offensive against Germany and Japan during World War II. He himself was a veteran pilot who had served in a pursuit squadron in France during World War I. He also won the Distinguished Flying Cross (1929) for staying aloft 150 hours in the airplane *Question Mark*—setting a new endurance record.

SPELLMAN, FRANCIS JOSEPH

Born: May 4, 1889, Whitman, Mass. Graduated, Fordham (1911). Ordained, Rome (1916). Auxiliary Bishop, Boston (1932). Archbishop, N.Y. (1939).

Archbishop Spellman became a cardinal of the Roman Catholic Church in 1946. He was appointed by Pope Pius XII, an old friend who had been Papal Secretary of State when Cardinal Spellman was the first American priest to be a member of the Secretariat. This is the department in charge of church relations with political governments.

SPERRY, ELMER AMBROSE

Born: Oct. 12, 1860, Cortland, N.Y. Died: June 16, 1930, Brooklyn, N.Y. Attended Cortland State Normal School and Cornell U.

Elmer Sperry was an inventor. He thought up the gyrocompass (a compass governed by a gyroscope so that it always points to true North), a compound internal-combustion engine, airplane and ship stabilizers (also using the gyroscope principle), fire-control apparatus, and a 1,500,000,000 candlepower searchlight, which is the most powerful ever devised.

SPRUANCE, RAYMOND AMES

Born: July 3, 1886, Baltimore, Md. Graduated, U.S. Naval Academy (1907). Admiral (1944). Retired (1948).

Admiral Spruance was one of the naval heroes of World War II. He was a task force commander at the crucial Battle of Midway (June, 1942), in which American sea and air forces beat back a Japanese thrust toward Hawaii. Spruance became head of the Central Pacific command (1943-44) and led the offensives against the Gilbert and Marshall Islands (1942). He was commander of the U.S. 5th Fleet when the war ended and acted as commander in chief of the U.S. Pacific Fleet (1945-46) before his retirement.

STANFORD, LELAND

Leland Stanford

Born: Mar. 9, 1824, Watervliet, N.Y. Died: June 21, 1893, Palo Alto, Cal. Studied law, Albany, N.Y.; admitted to N.Y. bar (1848). Governor of Cal. (1861-63). U.S. senator (1885-93).

Leland Stanford went to Cal. in 1852 and made a fortune selling miner's tools to the forty-niners looking for gold. He helped finance construction of the Central Pacific R.R., the Western end of the first transcontinental line, and was its president and director (1863-93). He was also instrumental in getting the Southern Pacific R.R. built and was its president (1885-90).

He founded Stanford U. at Palo Alto, Cal. (1885) in memory of his son, Leland, Jr., who died in 1884, aged five.

STANLEY, WENDELL MEREDITH

Born: Aug. 16, 1904, Ridgeville, Ind. Graduated, Earlham Coll., Ind., B.S. (1926); U. of Illinois, M.S. (1927), Ph. D. (1929). Studied in Munich, Germany (1930-31). Associated with

Rockefeller Institute for Medical Research, Princeton, N.J. (1931-48).

During his years with the Rockefeller Institute, Wendell Stanley distinguished himself when he became the first man to isolate a virus (the tobacco mosaic virus). The achievement was extremely important to the study of diseases, and for the contribution Stanley was awarded a Nobel prize in chemistry (1946), which he shared with J. H. Northrop and J. B. Sumner. Stanley also has made noteworthy studies of other viruses, including the once deadly disease, influenza.

He is now affiliated with the U. of California, where in 1948 he organized and became director of a special laboratory for virus research. He is also a professor of biochemistry there.

STANTON, EDWIN McMASTERS

Born: Dec. 19, 1814, Steubenville, O. Died: Dec. 24, 1869, Washington, D.C. Graduated, Kenyon Coll., O. (1836). Admitted to the bar (1837). U.S. Attorney General (1860-61).

In January, 1862, Abraham Lincoln chose Edwin M. Stanton as his Secretary of War to replace Simon Cameron. Stanton, a noted attorney, was sharp-tongued and short-tempered, but also honest, energetic, and capable. He ran the War Department well. After Lincoln's death, Stanton had a political feud with President Andrew Johnson, who tried to remove him from office (1868). The tangled chain of events led to the President's impeachment trial. When Johnson was acquitted (May, 1868), Stanton resigned. He received an appointment to the U.S. Supreme Court on December 20, 1869, but died four days later.

STANTON, ELIZABETH CADY

Born: Nov. 12, 1815, Johnstown, N.Y. Died: Oct. 26, 1902, New York City. First president of the National Woman Suffrage Association (1865-93).

Mrs. Stanton championed women's rights. She called the first meeting ever held in the U.S. on women's position in society. She met Susan B. Anthony in 1851 and was her longtime associate in the fight for women's privilege to vote. Mrs. Stanton also wanted equal educational advantages for women, equal property rights, more sensible divorce laws.

Lincoln Steffens

STEFFENS, JOSEPH LINCOLN

Born: Apr. 6, 1866, San Francisco, Cal. Died: Aug. 9, 1936, Carmel, Cal. Graduated, U. of California (1889). Managing editor, McClure's Magazine (1902-06). Associate editor, American Magazine and Everybody's (1906-11).

Lincoln Steffens was a "muckraking" journalist who exposed the graft and corruption he found in American politics and business. With such fellow crusaders as Upton Sinclair and Ida M. Tarbell, he was responsible for arousing interest in new social legislation. His best-known work is *Autobiography* (1931).

STEICHEN, EDWARD

Born: Mar. 27, 1879, Luxembourg. Lieutenant colonel, photo division of air service, World War I. Chief photographer, Condé Nast Publications (1923-38). Commander, U.S. Navy, World War II. Director, U.S. Navy Photographic Institute (1945). Retired at the rank of captain (1946).

Edward Steichen, who began his artistic career as a painter, has become a major influence in photography. With Alfred Stieglitz, he was one of the pioneers in evolving new photographic techniques and in the development of photography as an art. In 1954, he created the famous *Family of Man* photographic exhibit for New York City's Museum of Modern Art, for which he was director of the department of photography (1947-62).

STEINBECK, JOHN ERNST

Born: Feb. 27, 1902, Salinas, Cal.

John Steinbeck is one of America's important novelists. He first won recognition with *Tortilla Flat* in 1935 and achieved national prominence with *Of Mice and Men* (1937), which was also a successful stage play and motion picture. Perhaps his most famous book is *The Grapes of Wrath* (1939), a story of a family of migrant workers from the Dust Bowl area of the Midwest. It won a Pulitzer prize for fiction in 1940 and was made into a movie. Other Steinbeck works are: *In Dubious Battle* (1936), *The Long Valley* (1938), *The Pearl* (1947), *The Winter of Our Discontent* (1961), and *Travels With Charley* (1962).

In 1962 he was awarded the Nobel prize for literature.

John Steinbeck

STEINMETZ, CHARLES PROTEUS

Born: Apr. 9, 1865, Breslau, Germany. Died: Oct. 26, 1923, Schenectady, N.Y. Graduated, U. of Breslau; Harvard, A.M. (1902); Union Coll., N.Y., Ph.D. (1903). President, Board of Education, Schenectady, N.Y. (1912-23).

Charles Steinmetz had a scientific genius within a crippled, hunchbacked body. Educated in Germany as a mathematician, chemist, and electrical engineer, he fled to the U.S. in 1889, after being arrested for taking part in a Socialist uprising. He became a consulting engineer for the General Electric Co., at Schenectady, and eventually held some 200 patents for improvements in generators, motors, transformers, and other electrical apparatus. He made many studies of lightning and developed a lightning arrester for use on high-power transmission lines.

STEPHENS, ALEXANDER HAMILTON

Born: Feb. 11, 1812, near Crawfordville, Ga. Died: Mar. 4, 1883, Atlanta, Ga. Graduated, U. of Georgia (1832). Admitted Ga. bar (1834). Member, state legislature (1836-42). U.S. congressman (1843-59, 1873-82).

Alexander H. Stephens, vice-president of the Confederate States of America, stood by his native state of Ga. when she seceded from the Union (1861), even though he was opposed to secession. After the war, he was arrested and imprisoned for five months in Fort Warren (Boston, Mass.), but he was released later without a trial.

From 1871-73, Stephens was editor and part owner of the Atlanta *Southern Sun*. He was then returned to Congress, and in 1882, he was elected governor of Ga., a term cut short by his death.

Charles Steinmetz

STERNBERG, GEORGE MILLER

Born: June 8, 1838, Otsego Co., N.Y. Died: Nov. 3, 1915, Washington, D.C. Coll. of Physicians and Surgeons, N.Y. (1860). Assistant surgeon, U.S. Army (1861). Surgeon general, U.S. Army (1893-1902).

Dr. Sternberg's first experience with military medicine came during the Civil War when he served with the Army of the Potomac. As surgeon general, he organized the Havana Yellow Fever Commission (1898) headed by Walter Reed, which discovered that yellow fever was transmitted by mosquitos. He established the army medical school, dental corps, and nurse corps. A scientist as well as administrator, he demonstrated the organisms of malaria (1885), tuberculosis (1880), and typhoid fever (1886).

STEVENS, JOHN

Born: 1749, New York City. Died: Mar. 6, 1838, Hoboken, N.J. Graduated, King's Coll. (now Columbia) (1768).

John Stevens helped to establish the U.S. patent laws (1790) and was one of the first inventors to receive patents under them. They were for a steam engine, a vertical steam boiler, and a bellows. In 1809 he built the *Phoenix,* the first seagoing steamship, which made a trip from New York City to Philadelphia, Pa.

In 1810, Stevens turned to railroads. He organized the Pennsylvania R.R. company in 1823, but could not raise the money to build the road. He did construct a pioneer locomotive, however (1825).

His eldest son, Robert Livingston Stevens

(1787-1856), was a mechanical engineer who invented a T-rail (or Stevens rail) which was widely used for railroad track. He also imported from England a locomotive which ran on the first steam railway line in N.J. (1831).

A second son, Edwin Stevens (1795-1868), pioneered in the building of ironclad warships and bequeathed both the land and the money with which Stevens Institute of Technology, N.J., was founded.

STEVENS, THADDEUS

Born: Apr. 4, 1792, Danville, Vt. Died: Aug. 11, 1868, Washington, D.C. Graduated, Dartmouth (1814). Studied law at York, Pa., and admitted to the Pa. bar (1816). Pa. legislature (1833-35, 1837, 1841). U.S. congressman (1849-53, 1859-68).

Thaddeus Stevens was so violently opposed to slavery that he defended runaway slaves in court without fee. During the Civil War, as a Republican congressman, Stevens was a leader of those who favored a harsh policy toward the South and was against Lincoln's plans for Reconstruction. As a result, Stevens differed with President Andrew Johnson over treatment of the South and was a prime mover in the impeachment of the President, although poor health kept him from actually taking part in the proceedings.

STEVENSON, ADLAI EWING

Born: Feb. 5, 1900, Los Angeles, Cal. Graduated, Princeton (1922); Northwestern U., LL.B. (1926). Admitted to Ill. bar; practiced in Chicago (1927-33, 1935-41). Assistant to Secretary of the Navy (1941-44). Member, U.S. delegation to United Nations Conference, San Francisco, Cal.(1945), to United Nations (1946).

Elected governor of Ill. (1948), Adlai E. Stevenson was twice Democratic presidential candidate (1952, 1956), losing to Dwight D. Eisenhower both times. In 1961, he was appointed U.S. ambassador to the United Nations.

STIEGLITZ, ALFRED

Born: Jan. 1, 1864, Hoboken, N.J. Died: Apr. 13, 1946. New York City.

Thaddeus Stevens

Adlai Stevenson

Sent abroad to study engineering, Alfred Stieglitz returned to the U.S. an outstanding photographer (1890). In 1905 he opened a gallery at 291 Fifth Avenue, New York City, where photography was displayed as fine art—and where the best of modern French painting was exhibited as well. From 1917 to 1925, Stieglitz concentrated on his own photography. He then opened the Intimate Gallery (1925-30) and An American Place (1930-46), and introduced to America such French painters as Cezanne, Braque, and such American painters as Max Weber, John Marin, and Georgia O'Keeffe (Mrs. Stieglitz) (1887——).

STIMSON, HENRY LEWIS

Born: Sept. 21, 1867, New York City. Died: Oct. 20, 1950, Huntington, Long Island, N.Y. Graduated, Yale, B.A. (1888); Harvard, M.A. (1889); Harvard Law School (1889-90). Practiced in New York City (1891-1906).

Henry L. Stimson was the first and only man to serve in the cabinets of four Presidents. He was President Taft's Secretary of War (1911), President Hoover's Secretary of State (1929-33), and Secretary of War again for President Franklin Roosevelt (1940-45) and for President Truman (1945).

He also served as a colonel of artillery in France with the A.E.F. during World War I, and he was governor general of the Philippine Islands (1927-29).

STONE, HARLAN FISKE

Born: Oct. 11, 1872, Chesterfield, N.H. Died: Apr. 22, 1946, Washington, D.C. Graduated, Amherst (1894) and Columbia Law School (1898). Professor, Columbia Law School (1902-05), dean (1910-23). U.S. Attorney General (1924-25).

Harlan Fiske Stone was appointed to the Supreme Court by President Coolidge in 1925 and was Chief Justice from 1942-46. In his early days on the Court, Stone was known for his dissenting opinions. After 1933 he generally supported the measures of the New Deal.

STONE, LUCY

Born: Aug. 13, 1818, West Brookfield, Mass. Died: Oct. 18, 1893, Dorchester, Mass.

A leader in the struggle for women's rights, Lucy Stone married Henry Brown Blackwell in 1855, but insisted upon retaining her maiden name to show her equality as a partner in the marriage. Because women did not have the right to vote, Miss Stone refused to pay taxes on property she owned in N.J., claiming that it was "taxation without representation."

A brilliant lecturer, she spent her life actively fighting to gain social equality for women and was often able to sway audiences hostile to her sentiments. She also spoke avidly for the abolition of slavery.

STORY, JOSEPH

Born: Sept. 18, 1779, Marblehead, Mass. Died: Sept. 10, 1845, Cambridge, Mass. Graduated, Harvard (1798). Member, Mass. state legislature (1805-08). U.S. congressman (1808-09). Professor of law, Harvard (1829-45).

Henry L. Stimson

Harriet Beecher Stowe

Gilbert Stuart

Joseph Story was appointed to the Supreme Court bench in 1811, when he was thirty-two years old—the youngest person ever to hold that position. He served with John Marshall and shared many of the Chief Justice's strong opinions on the law. Story, whose term ran to 1845, was a major influence on American legal thought. Many of his discussions of various aspects of the law are still consulted. His most important published work was *Commentaries on the Constitution of the United States* (1833).

STOWE, HARRIET BEECHER

Born: June 14, 1811, Litchfield, Conn. Died: July 1, 1896, Hartford, Conn.

Harriet Beecher Stowe, sister of the Reverend Henry Ward Beecher, won an international reputation with her antislavery novel, *Uncle Tom's Cabin,* published in 1852. Within a year it sold 300,000 copies.

The book expressed the moral objections of many Northerners to slavery, but aroused great resentment in the South. During the Civil War, President Lincoln, meeting Mrs. Stowe for the first time, is reputed to have said, "So you're the little lady who wrote the book that started this big war!"

STUART, GILBERT

Born: Dec. 3, 1755, North Kensington, R.I. Died: July 9, 1828, Boston, Mass.

Gilbert Stuart is a painter known principally for his portraits of George Washington. He showed signs of talent early in his life, but he had little training until, at the age of twenty-one, he became a pupil of Benjamin West in London. His work abroad included portraits of many notable people, and he soon became the major American painter of his day.

Returning to the U.S. in 1792, he worked in New York City, Philadelphia, Pa., and Boston, Mass., and painted a gallery of famous Americans, among them General Henry Knox, Joseph Story, Oliver Hazard Perry, John Trumbull, and the first five Presidents of the U.S. He did several studies of Washington. Today his works can be seen at the Pennsylvania Academy of Fine Arts, Boston's Museum of Fine Arts, and the Metropolitan Museum in New York City.

Louis Sullivan *Charles Sumner*

SULLIVAN, LOUIS HENRI

Born: Sept. 3, 1856, Boston, Mass. Died: Apr. 14, 1924, Chicago, Ill. Attended Massachusetts Institute of Technology (1872-73) and the École des Beaux Arts, Paris (1874).

Although Louis Sullivan had few followers in his day, most of today's architects adhere to the principle laid down by him. The outward form of a structure, he said, should express its purpose or function, and he realized this concept in the buildings he designed.

He was among the first architects to use steel skeletons for his buildings, and to create skyscrapers. Among his followers was his pupil Frank Lloyd Wright.

SUMNER, CHARLES

Born: Jan. 6, 1811, Boston, Mass. Died: Mar. 11, 1874, Washington, D.C. Graduated, Harvard (1830), Harvard Law School (1833). Admitted to bar (1834). U.S. senator (1851-74).

Following a trip to Europe (1837-40), where he met leading pacifists, Charles Sumner became the spokesman in the U.S. for the outlawing of war. He was strongly opposed to the Mexican War, and in 1849 he called for a "congress of nations."

As a senator, he was passionately opposed to slavery and secession. An antislavery speech which he made in the Senate on May 20, 1856, provoked an irate Southern congressman, to attack him with a cane. He suffered injuries so severe that they kept him from carrying out his senatorial duties for nearly three years.

During and after the Civil War, he advocated harsh treatment of the South and demanded an end to slavery and equal suffrage for Negroes.

T

TAFT, ROBERT ALPHONSO

Born: Sept. 8, 1889, Cincinnati, Ohio. Died: July 31, 1953, New York City. Graduated, Yale (1910); Harvard, LL.B. (1913). Member, Ohio legislature (1921-26, 1931-32). U.S. senator (1939-53).

Robert A. Taft, the son of President William Howard Taft, was a leader of the conservative Republicans during his term as senator. He was an acknowledged expert on government taxes and finance. He opposed the New Deal, and was an isolationist, but favored U.S. participation in the United Nations.

He tried four times for the Republican presidential nomination, but lost once to Wendell Willkie (1940), twice to Thomas Dewey (1944, 1948), and once to Dwight Eisenhower (1952).

TAFT, WILLIAM HOWARD

Born: Sept. 15, 1857, Cincinnati, O. Died: Mar. 8, 1930, Washington, D.C. Graduated, Yale (1878); Cincinnati Law School (1880). Dean, Cincinnati Law School (1898-1900). Judge, O. superior court (1887-90). U.S. solicitor general (1890-92). U.S. circuit court judge (1892-1900). President, U.S. Philippine Commission (1900-01). First U.S. civil governor of Philippines (1901-04). Secretary of War (1904-08). Professor, constitutional law, Yale (1913-21). Chief Justice, Supreme Court (1921-30).

William Howard Taft, the twenty-sixth President of the U.S., is the only man to have been both Chief Executive and Chief Justice. He had extensive training and experience in the law, and an excellent record as an administrator. As governor of the Philippines, he was particularly successful in developing good relations between the islands and the U.S.

After serving as President Theodore Roosevelt's Secretary of War, he was hand-picked by T.R. as the Republican presidential candidate in 1908. He won election, defeating William Jennings Bryan. His term was marked by the establishment of the Labor Department (1911), the U.S. postal savings bank (1910), and parcel-post service (1912).

Taft was renominated in 1912, but was defeated in a three-cornered race with Theodore Roosevelt and Woodrow Wilson.

In 1921 he was appointed Chief Justice by President Harding.

TANEY, ROGER BROOKE

Born: Mar. 17, 1777, Calvert Co., Md. Died: Oct. 12, 1864, Washington, D.C. Graduated, Dickinson Coll., Md. (1795). Admitted to bar (1799); practiced in Frederick, Md. (1801-23). State legislator (1799-1800). State senator (1816-21). Md. attorney general (1827-31). U.S. Attorney General (1831-33). Appointed Secretary of the Treasury (1833).

Roger B. Taney (*Taw*-ny) succeeded John Marshall as Chief Justice of the U.S. Supreme Court in 1836 and served until 1864. It was during his term on the bench that the Court issued the memorable Dred Scott decision (1857), which held that the Negro was not a citizen and, therefore, had no right to sue in the Federal courts. In view of the rising antislavery feeling at the time, the decision is now regarded as having hastened the outbreak of the Civil War.

Robert A. Taft

William Howard Taft

Booth Tarkington

Deems Taylor

TARBELL, IDA MINERVA

Born: Nov. 5, 1857, Erie Co., Pa. Died: Jan. 6, 1944, Bridgeport, Conn. Allegheny Coll., Pa., B.A. (1880), M.A. (1883).

Ida Tarbell, like Upton Sinclair and Lincoln Steffens, was a crusading reporter of the economic and social ills of the U.S. A staff writer for *McClure's Magazine* (1894-1906) and the *American* (1906-15), she conducted investigations of industry, the most famous of which became her *History of the Standard Oil Company* (1904).

TARKINGTON, (Newton) BOOTH

Born: July 29, 1869, and Died: May 19, 1946, Indianapolis, Ind. Graduated, Purdue U. and Princeton. Member, Ind. legislature (1902-03).

One of America's leading fiction writers, Booth Tarkington won recognition with his first novel, *The Gentleman from Indiana* (1899). He followed this initial success with a number of popular novels and plays dealing charmingly and amusingly with American life and character at the turn of the century. He was twice awarded the Pulitzer prize: for *The Magnificent Ambersons* (1918) and *Alice Adams* (1921).

Tarkington's best-loved books are his humorous novels about growing up in Ind., among them *Penrod* (1914) and *Seventeen* (1916).

TAYLOR, (Joseph) DEEMS

Born: Dec. 22, 1885, New York City. Graduated, New York U. (1906). Music critic, New York World *(1921-25). Editor,* Musical America *(1927-29). Music consultant, Columbia Broadcasting System (from 1933). Intermission commentator for N.Y. Philharmonic broadcasts (1936-43).*

Deems Taylor is an outstanding musician and musical interpreter. His best-known orchestral work is *Through the Looking Glass* (1919); he is also the composer of two operas: *The King's Henchman* (1927), with a libretto (text) by the poetess Edna St. Vincent Millay, and *Peter Ibbetson* (1931). He is also well and warmly regarded for his musical commentaries, many of which have been collected in his several books: *Of Men and Music* (1937), *The Well-tempered Listener* (1940), and *Music to My Ears* (1949).

Zachary Taylor

Nikola Tesla

TAYLOR, ZACHARY

Born: Nov. 24, 1784, Montebello, Va. Died: July 9, 1850, Washington, D.C. Promoted to major general (1846).

Zachary Taylor, twelfth President of the U.S. spent forty years in the U.S. Army before becoming the nation's chief executive (1848). A hero of the Mexican War (1845-47), Taylor —called "Old Rough and Ready" by his soldiers—was the Whig party nominee. He took office on March 4, 1849, but died suddenly a year later and was succeeded by Vice-President Millard Fillmore. During his brief term in office, Taylor opposed the spread of slavery.

TELLER, EDWARD

Born: Jan. 15, 1908, Budapest, Hungary. Graduated, U. of Leipzig, Ph.D. (1930). Emigrated to U.S. (1935); naturalized citizen (1941). Professor of physics, George Washington U. (1935-41), U. of Chicago (1945-52), U. of California (since 1952).

Edward Teller, known as "the architect of the H-bomb," fled Germany (1933) after Hitler came to power. During World War II he worked at Columbia U. on atomic-bomb research. He was in charge of theoretical planning for the hydrogen bomb, produced and exploded the first one, and is in charge of the H-bomb laboratory at Livermore, Cal.

TESLA, NIKOLA

Born: July 9, 1857, Smiljan, Austria-Hungary. Died: Jan. 7, 1943, New York City. Educated at Karlstadt, Gratz, and the U. of Prague. Emigrated to U.S. (1884); naturalized citizen (1889).

Nikola Tesla was an inventor who made many contributions to the fields of radio transmission and electricity. Among his many inventions are an alternating-current motor (1888) and the Tesla coil or transformer (1891). He also perfected an arc lighting system (1886), incandescent lamps, and different types of electric generators. He developed an interest in the transmission of electric power without wires

THOMAS, GEORGE HENRY

Born: July 31, 1816, Southampton Co., Va. Died: Mar. 28, 1870, San Francisco, Cal. Graduated, West Point (1840).

Although George Thomas was a Southerner by birth, he remained loyal to the Union during the Civil War. A veteran of the fighting in Mexico, he was commissioned a brigadier general of volunteers (1861) when the Civil War began. An excellent officer, Thomas commanded the XIV Corps at the Battle of Chickamauga, Ga. (September, 1863), where the Union army was routed except for his troops. The stand he made to cover the Union withdrawal earned him the nickname the "Rock of Chickamauga." He led the Army of the Cumberland at Chattanooga, Tenn. (November, 1863) and against Atlanta, Ga. (1864). In December, 1864, he routed John Hood's army to win the Battle of Nashville, Tenn.

THOMAS, ISAIAH

Born: Jan. 30, 1750, Boston, Mass. Died: Apr. 4, 1831, Worcester, Mass.

Isaiah Thomas, publisher of the *Massachusetts Spy*, was a leading patriot of the American Revolution. He fought at both Lexington and Concord.

After the war, he published textbooks, law books, and more than one hundred children's books. He printed the first dictionary in the U.S. and America's first Bible in English.

THOREAU, HENRY DAVID

Born: July 12, 1817, and Died: May 6, 1862, Concord, Mass. Graduated, Harvard (1837). Taught school intermittently (1837-43).

Henry David Thoreau (Thaw-*ro*) was a

Henry David Thoreau

poet, essayist, naturalist, and social critic. From July 4, 1845, to September 6, 1847, he lived alone in a hut he built on the shore of Walden Pond at Concord, Mass. There he studied nature, wrote in peaceful solitude, and demonstrated his philosophy that life can be happy, admirable, and harmonious if man simplifies his world and reduces his needs to essentials. His experiences and reflections are contained in his book, *Walden* (1854).

Earlier (1843), his refusal to pay a Mass. poll tax, which he regarded as unfair, resulted in his arrest and a night in jail. On this occasion he wrote a famous essay, "Civil Disobedience." Later in life, Thoreau became an ardent abolitionist.

His other writings include: *A Week on the Concord and Merrimack Rivers* (1849), *Excursions* (1863), *The Maine Woods* (1864), *Cape Cod* (1865), and *A Yankee in Canada* (1866).

THORNDIKE, EDWARD LEE

Born: Aug. 31, 1871, Williamsburg, Mass. Died: Aug. 9, 1949, Montrose, N.Y. Graduated, Wesleyan, Conn. (1895); Harvard (1896); Columbia, Ph.D. (1898). Instructor, Western Reserve (1898-99). Professor, Teachers Coll., Columbia (1899-1941).

Edward L. Thorndike was a psychologist (a student of the mind, and of consciousness and behavior). He devised a number of new methods for measuring intelligence and the ability to learn. Many of them were used by the U.S. Army during World War I, and set a pattern for employment, placement, and educational guidance tests in postwar industry. Thorndike also conducted studies in vocabulary, which resulted in special dictionaries for children and young adults.

THORNTON, WILLIAM

Born: May 27, 1759, Tortola, British West Indies. Died: Mar. 28, 1828, Washington, D.C. Studied medicine, Edinburgh (1781-84); Aberdeen, M.D. (1784). Emigrated to U.S. (1787); naturalized citizen (1788). Commissioner of Patents (1802-28).

Although he never formally studied architecture, Dr. Thornton gained a knowledge of it in the course of his travels through Europe. He entered and won the competition for a plan for the U.S. Capitol in 1792—his design was chosen by George Washington. From 1794 to 1802, Thornton was a commissioner of the District of Columbia and supervised the construction of one wing of the Capitol. Benjamin Latrobe and others completed the structure, but remained basically faithful to Thornton's original design.

THURBER, JAMES GROVER

Born: Dec. 8, 1894, Columbus, O. Died: Nov. 2, 1961, New York City.

James Thurber was a humorist. His stories, essays, and cartoons appeared for many years in the *New Yorker* magazine, and in a succession of books. Among his works are: *The Seal in the Bedroom* (1932), *My Life and Hard Times* (1934), *The Middle-aged Man on the Flying Trapeze* (1935), *The Thurber Carnival* (1945); a children's book, *The 13 Clocks* (1950); a play, *The Male Animal* (with Elliott Nugent) (1939).

James Thurber

TICKNOR, WILLIAM DAVIS

Born: Aug. 6, 1810, Lebanon, N.H. Died: Apr. 10, 1864, Philadelphia, Pa.

William Ticknor was a Boston bookseller and publisher whose firm, Ticknor & Fields, printed the *Atlantic Monthly* and the works of most of the outstanding American writers of the 19th century. Emerson, Thoreau, Longfellow, Hawthorne, and Lowell were among its authors, and so were such great British poets as Robert Browning and Alfred Lord Tennyson. Ticknor also was the first American publisher to pay foreign authors for the rights to publish their work.

TILDEN, SAMUEL JONES

Born: Feb. 9, 1814, New Lebanon, N.Y. Died: Aug. 4, 1886, Greystone, N.Y. Attended Yale (1834). Graduated, New York U. Law School (1841). Elected, N.Y. legislature (1845, 1872). Helped to found the N.Y. Bar Association. Governor, N.Y. (1875-76).

One of the leading Democratic-party politicians of his day, Samuel Jones Tilden was a reformer and a foe of graft and corruption. He helped smash the notorious ring of political gangsters led by William Marcy "Boss" Tweed, in New York City (1872).

In 1876 Tilden ran for President against Rutherford B. Hayes in one of the closest elections in American history. Tilden appeared to have won, with 184 electoral votes against 163 for Hayes. But twenty-two others were in doubt, and a congressional electoral commission awarded them all to Hayes, who thereby won by one electoral vote.

TRUMAN, HARRY S.

Born: May 8, 1884, Lamar, Mo. Artillery officer, World War I. Attended Kansas City School of Law (1923-25). Judge, Jackson Co., Mo. (1922-34). U.S. senator (1935-45).

Harry S. Truman, thirty-second President of the U.S., entered the White House on the death of President Franklin Roosevelt (April 12, 1945). He had worked on his father's farm, near Independence, Mo., entered Mo. politics, and served with distinction as U.S. senator. In 1944 he was elected as Roosevelt's fourth-term Vice-President.

He was elected to a second term as President in 1948, defeating Thomas E. Dewey in a surprising upset.

Harry Truman

His years as President were momentous ones: He made the decision to drop the atom bombs which brought World War II to an end. He established the Truman Doctrine to help nations threatened by communism (1947); Greece and Turkey were among the first to receive aid. Truman also pushed for acceptance of the European Recovery Program (Marshall Plan) to assist Allied nations that had been devastated by the war.

TRUMBULL, JOHN

Born: June 6, 1756, Lebanon, Conn. Died: Nov. 10, 1843, New York City.

Artist John Trumbull was one of three sons of Jonathan Trumbull (1710-85), a patriot during the Revolution and friend of George Washington. (Tradition says that the term "Brother Jonathan," meaning a typical American, comes from Washington's familiar name for the elder Trumbull.)

John Trumbull

John Trumbull studied painting with Benjamin West in England. By 1804 he had returned to the U.S. to paint portraits of Washington, John Adams, Jefferson, and other notable persons of the time. He also painted historical scenes, such as the *Battle of Bunker's Hill,* the *Signing of the Declaration of Independence,* and the *Surrender of Lord Cornwallis at Yorktown.* Congress commissioned (1817) four of his works for the rotunda of the Capitol at Washington, D.C.

A second son, Jonathan (1740-1809), was on Washington's staff, a congressman (1789-95), a senator (1795-96), and governor of Conn. (1797-1809). The third son, Joseph (1737-78), was a member of the Continental Congress (1774) and commissary general of the Continental army during the Revolution.

TUBMAN, HARRIET

Born: about 1820, Dorchester Co., Md. Died: 1913.

Harriet Tubman escaped from slavery (1849) to become a friend of the principal Northern abolitionists and a symbol of Negro freedom. As a "conductor" on the underground railroad, she helped to smuggle some 300 slaves to freedom in the Northern states and Canada. During the Civil War, in the guise of a nurse and laundress, she served as a Union spy.

TWAIN, MARK

(See Clemens, Samuel Langhorne.)

TYLER, JOHN

Born: Mar. 29, 1790, Greenway, Va. Died: Jan. 18, 1862, Richmond, Va. Graduated, William and Mary (1807). Admitted to Va. bar (1809). Va. state legislature (1811-16). U.S. congressman (1816-21). Governor of Va. (1825-27). U.S. senator (1827-36).

John Tyler, tenth President of the U.S., was the first man to become President by succession. He was elected as William Henry Harrison's Vice-President—with the campaign slogan, "Tippecanoe and Tyler too"—but soon found himself in the White House when Harrison died (April 4, 1841) one month after his inauguration. During Tyler's administration the boundary between the U.S. and Canada was settled and first steps were taken toward the annexation of Tex.

Although nominated for re-election, Tyler withdrew from the race and played no further role in politics until 1860, when he attempted to act as peacemaker after S.C.'s secession from the Union.

John Tyler

U

UREY, HAROLD CLAYTON

Born: Apr. 29, 1893, Walkerton, Ind. Graduated, U. of Montana, B.S. (1917); U. of California, Ph.D. (1923). Taught chemistry, Montana (1917-21); Johns Hopkins (1924-29); Columbia (1929-45); U. of Chicago (1945-58); U. of California (1958——).

Harold C. Urey was awarded the Nobel prize in chemistry (1934) for his discovery of deuterium or heavy hydrogen ("heavy" because its atomic weight is double that of ordinary hydrogen). He also has worked on the structure of atoms and molecules, and was a member of the Manhattan Project (1942-45), which produced the A-bomb.

Arthur H. Vandenberg

V

Martin Van Buren

VAN BUREN, MARTIN

Born: Dec. 5, 1782, and Died: July 24, 1862, Kinderhook, N.Y. Studied law and admitted to the N.Y. bar (1803). Practiced in Kinderhook (1803-09). State senator (1812-20). State attorney general (1815-19). U.S. senator (1821-28). Became governor of N.Y. (Jan., 1829); resigned (Mar., 1829).

Martin Van Buren, eighth President of the U.S., served from 1837-41. He was a steadfast friend of Andrew Jackson. His tact and good political sense, both as Secretary of State (1829-31) and as Vice-President (1833-37), helped Old Hickory over a number of rough spots.

Van Buren was a better politician than legislator, however. His own administration was marred by financial panic (1837) and disputes over the annexation of Tex. "Little Van" was defeated for a second term by William Henry Harrison.

VANDENBERG, ARTHUR HENDRICK

Born: Mar. 22, 1884, and Died: Apr. 18, 1951, Grand Rapids, Mich.

Arthur Vandenberg was appointed to the U.S. Senate to fill a vacancy in 1928 and served for twenty-three years. An isolationist before the U.S. entered World War II, Vandenberg later broadened his views and worked to establish the United Nations and the World Bank. As Republican chairman of the Senate Foreign Relations Committee (1948), he was influential in obtaining the Senate's approval of the European Recovery Program (Marshall Plan) and other international legislation.

VANDERBILT, CORNELIUS

Born: May 27, 1794, Port Richmond, Staten Island, N.Y. Died: Jan. 4, 1877, New York City.

Cornelius Vanderbilt—known as "Commodore"—was the founder of a family fortune earned from steamship and railroad lines. He quit school at eleven and had his own passenger and freight-boat service between New York and Staten Island by the time he was sixteen. (He married at nineteen and eventually fathered thirteen children.)

During the Cal. gold rush, he operated a passenger route across Nicaragua, in Central America, which shortened the trip between the East and West coasts for eager prospectors much as the Panama Canal does today. Vanderbilt next entered the transatlantic trade, and when the Civil War ended turned to railroading. He merged several lines into the New York Central R.R. and extended its service to Chicago, Ill.

At his death, the "Commodore" was worth $100,000,000.

VEBLEN, THORSTEIN BUNDE

Born: July 30, 1857, Cato, Wis. Died: Aug. 3, 1929, Palo Alto, Cal. Graduated, Carleton Coll., Minn. (1880); Yale, Ph.D. (1884); other postgraduate studies at Johns Hopkins and Cornell. Taught at U. of Chicago (1893-1906), Stanford (1906-09), U. of Missouri (1911-18), New School for Social Research, New York City (1918-20).

Thorstein Veblen was an economist and social scientist whose books analyzed and criticized American society. Although not popular in his own time, Veblen has since won respect for his insights. His most famous book is *The Theory of the Leisure Class* (1899), which discusses the values of America's middle class. *The Theory of Business Enterprise* (1904) outlines a society whose production and distribution are controlled by trained engineers.

Among his other writings are *The Instinct of Workmanship* (1914), *An Inquiry into the Nature of Peace* (1917), and *The Engineers and the Price System* (1921).

VOLSTEAD, ANDREW JOSEPH

Born: 1860, Goodhue Co., Minn. Died: Jan. 20, 1947, Granite Falls, Minn. Educated, St. Olaf Coll. Admitted to Minn. bar (1884), practiced law. U.S. congressman (1903-23).

Andrew Volstead sponsored legislation to enforce Prohibition. The so-called Volstead Act, passed in 1919 over President Wilson's veto, spelled out the ways the government intended to keep liquor from being made, sold, or distributed under the 18th Amendment. The act was nullified by repeal of the 18th Amendment in 1933.

Cornelius Vanderbilt

Thorstein Veblen

Robert F. Wagner

W

WAGNER, ROBERT FERDINAND

Born: June 8, 1877, Nastatten, Germany. Died: May 4, 1953, New York City. Graduated, Coll. of the City of New York (1891); New York Law School, LL.B. (1900). N.Y. state senator (1909-18). N.Y. supreme court (1919-26).

Robert F. Wagner was a U.S. senator from N.Y. (1927-49) elected on the Democratic ticket. He was a staunch supporter of President Franklin Roosevelt's New Deal program of domestic legislation. He originated the National Labor Relations Act (1936)—the so-called Wagner Act—which gave trade unions the right to organize and bargain collectively, without employer interference. He also was responsible for the Railroad Retirement Act (1934), which provided pensions for railway workers. He helped pass the Social Security Act in 1935.

A son, Robert, Jr. (1910——), was elected Mayor of New York City (1953) and currently holds that office.

WAINWRIGHT, JONATHAN MAYHEW

Born: Aug. 23, 1883, Walla Walla, Wash. Died: Sept. 2, 1953, San Antonio, Tex. Graduated, West Point (1906). Served with A.E.F. in France (1918). Received rank of major general (1940), general (1945).

Jonathan Mayhew Wainwright was the third of his name. His grandfather (1792-1854) was a Protestant Episcopal bishop of New York City; his father (1821-63) was a naval officer with Farragut and Porter during the Civil War. He himself—General Jonathan "Skinny" Wainwright—was the hero of Bataan and Corregidor in World War II.

Stationed in the Philippines when the Japanese struck in December, 1941, General Wainwright assumed command when General Douglas MacArthur was ordered to Australia. He conducted the hopeless defense of Bataan peninsula and the Manila Bay fortress of Corregidor with stubbornness and courage (March-May, 1942), and when the remaining American force on Corregidor was forced to surrender, he became a captive of the Japanese.

He was rescued from a Japanese prison camp in Manchuria (1945), witnessed Japan's surrender aboard the battleship *Missouri,* and was awarded the Congressional Medal of Honor for his heroism.

Jonathan M. Wainwright

WAIT, WILLIAM BELL

Born: Mar. 25, 1839, Amsterdam, N.Y. Died: Oct. 25, 1916, New York City. Principal, New York Institute for the Education of the Blind (1863-1905).

William Wait invented the "New York point system," a variation of Braille, for printing literature for the blind. In 1894 he produced a "kleidograph,"—a typewriter which could emboss the point system on paper. Later he constructed a "stereograph" for embossing it on metal printing plates.

WAITE, MORRISON REMICK

Born: Nov. 29, 1816, Lyme, Conn. Died: Mar. 23, 1888, Washington, D.C. Graduated, Yale (1837). Practiced law, Maumee and Toledo, Ohio. Member, Ohio legislature (1849-50). President, Ohio constitutional convention (1873-74).

Morrison R. Waite was appointed Chief Justice of the U.S. Supreme Court by President Grant in 1874. He presided for fourteen years over a Court which gave significant and long-lasting interpretations of the 14th and 15th Amendments to the Constitution. These were the so-called "Reconstruction Amendments" passed after the Civil War. Although written for all citizens, they were intended to guarantee civil and voting rights particularly for Negroes. They raised many difficult constitutional questions which the Waite Court boldly undertook to solve.

WAKSMAN, SELMAN ABRAHAM

Born: July 22, 1888, Prikula, Russia. Emigrated to U.S. (1910); naturalized citizen (1916). Graduated, Rutgers, B.S. (1915); U. of California, Ph.D. (1918). Teacher of soil microbiology, Rutgers (1918-58).

Selman Waksman, founder and director of Rutgers' Institute of Microbiology, was awarded a Nobel prize in 1952 for his discovery of streptomycin, an antibiotic "wonder drug" which has proved extremely valuable in treating many diseases.

WALD, LILLIAN D.

Born: Mar. 10, 1867, Cincinnati, O. Died: Sept. 1, 1940, Westport, Conn. Graduated, New York Hospital Training School for Nurses.

Lillian Wald was a social worker in New York City. In 1893 she organized a visiting-nurse service and in 1902 the first city school-nursing service. From her work developed the famous Henry Street Settlement. She also urged the organization of a U.S. Children's Bureau—an idea that was finally adopted by Congress in 1908.

WALLACE, HENRY AGARD

Born: Oct. 7, 1888, Adair Co., Ia. Graduated, Iowa State (1910). Associate editor (1910-24), editor (1924-29), Wallace's Farmer.

Henry A. Wallace entered President Frank-

Lillian Wald

Henry A. Wallace

lin Roosevelt's cabinet as Secretary of Agriculture in 1933. He was an agricultural scientist who had developed an excellent variety of hybrid corn. He also edited the influential agricultural journal, *Wallace's Farmer,* founded by his grandfather and carried on by his father.

Wallace was elected Vice-President in 1940, for Roosevelt's third term. He also served in the Truman cabinet as Secretary of Commerce (1945-46). He broke with the administration over foreign policy and was the Progressive party's unsuccessful presidential candidate in the election of 1948.

WALLACE, LEWIS (Lew)

Born: Apr. 10, 1827, Brookville, Ind. Died: Feb. 15, 1905, Crawfordsville, Ind. U.S. ambassador to Turkey (1881-85).

Lew Wallace wrote *Ben Hur* (1880) while serving as governor of the New Mexico Territory. Subtitled *A Tale of the Christ,* it told of the impact of Christianity on the lives and fortunes of its Jewish hero, Ben Hur, and Messala, his Roman friend turned enemy. Although Wallace wrote other novels—*The Fair God* (1873) and *The Prince of India* (1893)—none was as successful as his first.

Wallace's fame as an author, however, has somewhat obscured his career as soldier and diplomat. He served in the Mexican War and joined the Union army as a brigadier general at the outbreak of the Civil War (1861). Elevated to the rank of major general (1862), he fought in the battles of Fort Donelson, Shiloh, and Monocacy River.

WANAMAKER, JOHN

Born: July 11, 1838, and Died: Dec. 12, 1922, Philadelphia, Pa. U.S. Postmaster General (1889-93).

John Wanamaker became one of the nation's leading merchants through his awareness of the power of advertising and his development of the department store. He and a brother-in-law established their first store in Philadelphia in 1861. Eight years later it was the largest men's clothing store in the country, and by 1877 it had become a department store. Wanamaker was one of the first merchants to buy a large volume of advertising in newspapers and to pay large salaries to writers of advertising copy. Appointed Postmaster General by President Benjamin Harrison, he greatly improved the efficiency of postal services.

WARREN, EARL

Born: Mar. 19, 1891, Los Angeles, Cal. Graduated, U. of California (1914). District attorney, Alameda Co., Cal. (1925-39). Attorney general, Cal. (1939-43). Governor of Cal. (1943-53). Republican vice-presidential nominee (1948).

Earl Warren was appointed Chief Justice of the U.S. Supreme Court by President Eisenhower in 1953. In the period since then, the Court has decided a number of civil rights

Lew Wallace

Earl Warren

cases, most notably *Brown vs. the Board of Education of Topeka, Kan.* (1954), in which it held that segregation in public schools must be brought to an end.

WARREN, JOHN

Born: 1753, Roxbury, Mass. Died: 1815, Cambridge, Mass. Graduated, Harvard (1771). Practiced, Salem, Mass.

John Warren, like his patriot brother, Joseph, was an active participant in the American Revolution. A leading New England surgeon, he was present at the Boston Tea Party (1773) and served in the Continental army as a surgeon (1775-77). He was also a founder of the Harvard Medical School (1782) and its first professor of anatomy and surgery.

His son, John Collins Warren (1778-1856), was graduated from Harvard in 1797, was a teacher there from 1809-47, and dean of the medical school (1816-19). He was among the founders of Mass. General Hospital (1821) and performed the pioneer operation (1846) in which the patient was anesthetized by William Morton's ether preparation.

WARREN, JOSEPH

Born: June 11, 1741, Roxbury, Mass. Died: June 17, 1775, Boston, Mass. Graduated, Harvard (1759). Practiced medicine in Boston.

Prior to the American Revolution, Dr. Joseph Warren was a patriot leader in Mass. He sent Paul Revere off on his famous ride to Lexington and Concord (April, 1775), and was a major general of the Mass. militia. Warren fought at Bunker Hill (June 17, 1775) and was killed near the close of the battle.

WASHINGTON, BOOKER TALIAFERRO

Born: Apr. 5, 1856, Hale's Ford, Va. Died: Nov. 14, 1915, Tuskegee, Ala. Graduated, Hampton Institute, Va. (1875). Taught school (1875-77).

The son of a Negro slave and white father, Booker T. Washington worked his way through school at Malden, W. Va., by laboring

Booker T. Washington

in a salt furnace and coal mine. The foremost advocate of Negro education in the U.S., Washington organized (1881) a school at Tuskegee, Ala., to train Negroes in trades and professions. It became the outstanding Negro educational institution in the U.S. Washington wrote several books, of which the best known is *Up From Slavery* (1901), an autobiography.

WASHINGTON, GEORGE

Born: Feb. 22, 1732, Westmoreland Co., Va. Died: Dec. 13, 1799, Mount Vernon, Va. Married (1759), Martha Dandridge Custis (1731-1802). Member, Va. House of Burgesses (1759-74). Continental Congress (1774-75). Appointed commander in chief, Continental army (June 15, 1775). Dorchester Heights (Mar. 17, 1776). Battle of Long Island (Aug. 27-30, 1776), Trenton (Dec. 25, 1776), Princeton (Jan. 3, 1777), Brandywine (Sept. 11, 1777), Germantown (Oct. 4, 1777), Monmouth (June 28, 1778), Yorktown (Oct. 19, 1781). President, Constitutional Convention (1787). First President of U.S. (1789-97).

George Washington, first President of the U.S., was the "Father of His Country." He was a gentleman planter who loved his Mount

Vernon home, but saw little of it through eight years of warfare as commander in chief of the Continental army and eight years as President.

As a young man he was a surveyor and an officer of the Va. militia; he fought (1755-59) in the French and Indian War and rose to the rank of lieutenant colonel. He was a leader in the movement for independence from Great Britain, and shortly after the Revolutionary War began at Lexington and Concord, he was appointed commander in chief. He planned and fought with resolution and valor, despite often overwhelming odds. When the war ended (1783), Washington bade his officers farewell (at Fraunces Tavern, New York City) and retired to Mount Vernon.

He was recalled to be a member of the Va. delegation to the Constitutional Convention (1787), at which he presided. And he was influential in getting the resulting U.S. Constitution adopted by the states.

In 1789 he was inaugurated first President. His two terms were difficult ones, but by his dignity and good sense he did much to establish the office of President as the democratic institution it is today.

WAYNE, ANTHONY

Born: Jan. 1, 1745, Chester Co., Pa. Died: Dec. 15, 1796, Presque Isle, Pa. Member, Pa. legislature (1784). Elected U.S. congressman from Ga. (1791-92).

Anthony Wayne, whose daring on the battlefield earned him the nickname "Mad Anthony," fought all through the Revolution. His greatest feat was the capture of the British

George Washington

stronghold at Stony Point, N.Y. (1779), by a brilliantly led night attack.

After the Revolution, Wayne conducted a campaign against hostile Indians in the Ohio Territory and decisively defeated them at Fallen Timbers (1794). Afterward, he arranged a peace treaty which permitted settlement of vast regions west of the Ohio River.

WEBSTER, DANIEL

Born: Jan. 18, 1792, Salisbury (now Franklin), N.H. Died: Oct. 24, 1852, Marshfield, Mass. Graduated, Dartmouth (1801). Studied law and admitted to bar (1805). U.S. congressman from N.H. (1813-17), from Mass. (1823-27). U.S. senator (1827-41, 1845-50). Secretary of State (1841-43, 1850-52).

One of America's great orators, Daniel Webster distinguished himself both as a statesman and a constitutional lawyer. His several appearances before the Supreme Court (1818-24) not only were victorious for Webster and his clients, but produced important constitutional interpretations as well.

During his years in Congress and the Senate, Webster proved himself an important leader among the politicians of his day. He is best remembered for those occasions on which he used his political strength and his great gift as a public speaker to insure the preservation of the Union. The first challenge came when S.C. threatened secession (1828) over an unfavorable tariff law. Webster exposed the impossibilities of S.C.'s plan, declaring: "Liberty and Union, now and forever, one and inseparable!" In a second instance, he put aside his own passionate antislavery beliefs to gain the passage of the Compromise of 1850, hoping it would save the nation during the stormy years before the Civil War. "I . . . speak today," he said, "not as a Massachusetts man, nor a northern man, but as an American. . . ."

WEBSTER, NOAH

Born: Oct. 16, 1758, West Hartford, Conn. Died: May 28, 1843, New Haven, Conn. Graduated, Yale (1778). Studied law and admitted to Conn. bar (1781). Editor and journalist, N.Y. (1793-1803).

Noah Webster compiled the first American

Anthony Wayne

Daniel Webster

Noah Webster (teaching)

dictionary. *Webster's Spelling Book*—more often called the *Blue-Backed Speller*—appeared in 1783 and was a first attempt to standardize American (as opposed to British) pronunciations and spellings of the English language. Eventually, Webster added a grammar and a reader to his speller, the whole being called *A Grammatical Institute of the English Language*. The speller was necessary and popular; by 1890 its sales exceeded 70,000,000 copies.

WEEMS, MASON LOCKE

Born: 1759, Anne Arundel Co., Md. Died: May 23, 1825, Beaufort, S.C. Ordained, Anglican minister (1784). Held pastorate in Md. (1784-92). Traveling bookseller (1794-1824).

"Parson" Weems was the author of *The Life and Memorable Actions of George Washington* (1800), one of whose editions contained the heart-warming but false story that youthful George had cut down a cherry tree. ("I cannot tell a lie. I did it with my little hatchet.")

The "Parson" also wrote biographies of Benjamin Franklin, William Penn, and Francis Marion, and uplifting moral tracts.

WEST, BENJAMIN

Born: Oct. 10, 1783, Springfield, Pa. Died: Mar. 11, 1820, London, England.

Benjamin West was an important American painter who spent the greater part of his career in London. He settled there in 1763, after work

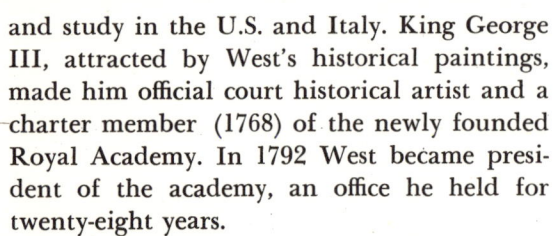

Benjamin West   *James Whistler*

and study in the U.S. and Italy. King George III, attracted by West's historical paintings, made him official court historical artist and a charter member (1768) of the newly founded Royal Academy. In 1792 West became president of the academy, an office he held for twenty-eight years.

He was a generous and helpful instructor of young American artists. Among his students were Samuel Morse, Gilbert Stuart, Charles Willson Peale, and John Singleton Copley.

His more outstanding works include *The Death of Wolfe, Death on the Pale Horse, Christ Healing the Sick,* and *Penn's Treaty with the Indians.*

WESTINGHOUSE, GEORGE

Born: Oct. 6, 1846, Central Bridge, N.Y. Died: Mar. 12, 1914, New York City. Served, Union army (1863-64). Assistant engineer, U.S. Navy (1864-66).

An inventor with more than 400 patents to his credit, George Westinghouse began his career when he abandoned his studies at Union Coll., N.Y., to work in his father's machine shop. By the time he was twenty-two, he had obtained patents for a rotary steam engine and for a device for replacing derailed railroad coaches. The invention for which he is best known—the air brake—came in 1869. Its use on passenger trains made high-speed rail travel safe, and its quick acceptance led Westinghouse to organize the Westinghouse Air Brake Co. (1869).

Next, Westinghouse turned his talents to developing electrically controlled railroad signal switches, and set up a company (1882) for their manufacture. Later investigations led to the invention of shock absorbers, marine steam turbines, a trolley-car motor, an electrical brake for subway cars, and a system for controlling and transmitting gas over long distances. He also developed improved transformers and pioneered the use, in America, of the alternating-current system for transmitting electricity.

WHARTON, EDITH NEWBOLD

Born: Jan. 24, 1862, New York City. Died: Aug. 11, 1937, in France.

Edith Wharton did not begin writing seriously until she was almost forty years old, after her marriage to Edward Wharton (1885) had ended. Her first volume of short stories was published in 1899, her first novel, *The Valley of Decision*, in 1902. Success came in 1905, when she completed *The House of Mirth*. In this, as in subsequent works, she revealed and analyzed American society in an adept and fine prose style.

Her writings include: *Ethan Frome* (1911), *The Age of Innocence* (1920), which won the Pulitzer prize (1921), and many short stories.

WHISTLER, JAMES ABBOTT McNEILL

Born: July 10, 1834, Lowell, Mass. Died: July 17, 1903, London, England.

A masterful etcher, engraver, and painter, James McNeill Whistler is best known for his *Portrait of My Mother*. Most of his work was done abroad—in Paris (1858-70) and London (from 1870). His paintings show the influence of the Spanish master, Velasquez, and of Japanese art. He emphasizes color and the arrangement of color rather than form. Among his canvases are *The White Girl, Peacock Room,* and a portrait of Thomas Carlyle.

WHITE, ANDREW DICKSON

Born: Nov. 7, 1832, Homer, N.Y. Died: Nov. 4, 1918, Ithaca, N.Y. Graduated, Yale (1853). Attaché to U.S. Legation, Petersburg, Russia (1854-55). N.Y. state senator (1864-67). Minister to Germany (1879-81), to Russia (1892-94). Ambassador to Germany (1897-1902).

Although he served his country many times in the field of foreign affairs, it was as an educator that Andrew Dickson White made his chief contributions. A co-founder of Cornell, he served as that university's first president (1867-85) and was a teacher in its history department. While there, he increased in number and type the courses of study offered by the school, adding a broad program in humanities and natural sciences to those in agriculture and the mechanical arts.

WHITE, EDWARD DOUGLASS

Born: Nov. 3, 1845, Lafourche parish, La. Died: May 19, 1921, Washington, D.C. Educated, Jesuit Coll., New Orleans, and Georgetown U. Served in Confederate army (1861-63). Judge, state supreme court (1879). U.S. senator (1891-94).

Edward D. White was appointed an associate justice of the U.S. Supreme Court by President Cleveland in 1896 and Chief Justice by President Taft in 1910. The first Southerner to become Chief Justice since Roger Taney, White was usually conservative in his decisions.

WHITE, ELWYN BROOKS

Born: 1899, Mt. Vernon, N.Y. Graduated, Cornell (1921).

E. B. White, long-time member of the staff of the *New Yorker* magazine, is an essayist notable for wit, keen observation, and faultless literary style. Two volumes of his essays have appeared under the titles *One Man's Meat* (1942) and *The Wild Flag* (1946). He also has written *Stuart Little* (1945), a story for children, and edited (with his wife, Katherine S. White) *The Subtreasury of American Humor* (1941).

WHITMAN, WALT

Born: May 31, 1819, Huntington, Long Island, N.Y. Died: Mar. 26, 1892, Camden, N.J.

Known as the "Good Gray Poet," Walt Whitman was the voice of American democracy. He saw its strength and merit in the common man, whom he praised again and again in his poetry.

The finest example of this appears in *Leaves of Grass*—a work of genius, in which Whitman ably evokes from his free and unique verse form the spirit of liberty and individuality he

Walt Whitman

found in his nation's people. It was the first collection of the poet's work, and he not only published it himself, but set the type for it, and later wrote anonymous reviews to promote it. (Six more editions, with Whitman's revisions and additions were published between 1856-81.)

Before the publication of *Leaves of Grass*, Whitman worked at varying times as a printer's devil, schoolteacher, and carpenter, writing and publishing poetry in his spare time. He also wrote free-lance articles for the *Democratic Review* and the *Columbian Magazine*, and was both editor and reporter for the Brooklyn *Daily Eagle* (1846-48), the New Orleans *Crescent* (1848), and the Brooklyn *Freeman* (1848-49).

At the outbreak of the Civil War, the poet served the Union as a volunteer nurse, working in hospitals at the front after 1862.

Other works by him include *Drum Taps* (1865) (which contains the memorable "When Lilacs Last in the Dooryard Bloom'd"), *Passage to India* (1871), *Goodbye My Fancy* (1891), and *The Wound-Dresser* (1898).

WHITNEY, ELI

Born: Dec. 8, 1765, Westboro, Mass. Died: Jan. 8, 1825, New Haven, Conn. Graduated, Yale (1792).

Eli Whitney was the inventor of the cotton gin, a machine for separating cotton fibers from seeds. He had set his mind to the problem at the request of Mrs. Nathanael Greene, the widow of the Revolutionary War general, whom he was visiting near Savannah, Ga. He devised the gin within ten days (1793). What had once been a slow, laborious hand process could now be done with speed and ease; the cotton industry boomed as a result.

Whitney's gin was widely imitated before he could get a patent and he never made much from the invention. In 1798 he opened a firearms factory in New Haven, Conn. He designed interchangeable parts, so that his arms could be assembled on a mass-production basis.

WHITNEY, JOSIAH DWIGHT

Born: Nov. 23, 1819, Northampton, Mass. Died: Aug. 18, 1896, Lake Sunapee, N.H. Graduated, Yale (1839). Studied abroad (1842-47). Professor of geology, Harvard (1865).

Josiah Whitney and his brother William Collins (1841-1904) both rendered important services to their nation. Josiah, who proved himself a brilliant economist as well as a geologist, devoted much of his life to studying the mineral content of the soil in various parts of the U.S.—areas around Lake Superior and in Ia., Ill., and Wis. His findings made wiser exploitation of America's resources possible.

William Whitney, also a graduate of Yale (1863), was appointed Secretary of the Navy (1885) by Grover Cleveland. While in that capacity, he helped to secure legislation for the manufacture of armor-plated war vessels.

WHITTIER, JOHN GREENLEAF

Born: Dec. 17, 1807, Haverhill, Mass. Died: Sept. 7, 1892, Hampton Falls, Mass. Mass. legislature (1834-35).

John Greenleaf Whittier was a self-educated poet and a vigorous abolitionist. He is best remembered for his poetic pictures of New England life, found in *Snow-Bound* (1866), and "Maud Muller" (1867), and for other poems, such as "Barbara Frietchie," "The Barefoot Boy," and "Skipper Ireson's Ride."

WILKES, CHARLES

Born: Apr. 3, 1798, New York City. Died: Feb. 8, 1877, Washington, D.C. Admiral (1866).

Charles Wilkes commanded the first government-sponsored exploration of the Pacific Ocean (1838-42). His squadron of six ships traveled to South America, Samoa, the Fiji Islands, and Hawaii, while surveying and charting the Pacific. Wilkes Land, in the Antarctic,

Eli Whitney

John Greenleaf Whittier

is named after him; he sighted and claimed it for the U.S. in 1840.

During the Civil War, he was responsible for the "Trent affair." While commanding the U.S.S. *San Jacinto,* he halted the British packet steamer *Trent* (November 8, 1861) and removed two Confederate diplomats bound for England. The action almost brought Britain into the war on the side of the Confederacy. But Lincoln ordered the diplomats released—and Wilkes was thanked by Congress.

WILLARD, EMMA HART

Born: Feb. 23, 1787, Berlin, Conn. Died: Apr. 15, 1870, Troy, N.Y. Attended Berlin Academy, Conn. Headed Middlebury (Vt.) Female Academy (1907-09).

Emma Willard pioneered the struggle to gain equal education rights for women in the U.S. She began her fight by opening a school for girls in her home at Middlebury, Vt., in 1814. There she taught subjects never before offered to female students.

In 1818 she carried her movement to the N.Y. legislature. Her arguments before that body were so convincing that Governor De Witt Clinton invited her to move to N.Y. and the legislature granted her a charter to establish Waterford Academy (1819). Finally, in 1821 she founded Troy Female Seminary—later called the Emma Willard School. It was the first college-level school for women in the U.S.

In addition, Mrs. Willard wrote many history and geography textbooks and trained hundreds of teachers who spread her doctrines. She was also the author of a collection of poetry, including her best-known poem, "Rocked in the Cradle of the Deep."

WILLARD, FRANCES

Born: Sept. 28, 1839, Churchville, N.Y. Died: Feb. 18, 1898, New York City. Graduated, Northwestern Female Coll. (1859). President, Evanston Coll. for Ladies (1871-74).

A teacher, reformer, and temperance leader, Frances Willard was president of the National Woman's Christian Temperance Union (W.C.T.U.) from 1879-98, and of the World Wom-

Frances Willard

Wendell Willkie

an's Christian Temperance Union from 1887.

Miss Willard was also active in other reform movements, including the struggle to obtain voting rights for women.

WILLIAMS, ROGER

Born: About 1603, London, England. Died: 1683, Providence, R.I. Graduated, Cambridge (1627). Emigrated to Mass. (1631).

Roger Williams, the first champion of religious freedom in America, was expelled (1635) from Mass. by the Puritans because of religious and political differences with that colony's leaders. With some followers he founded Providence (1636), the first settlement in R.I. In 1639, he established the first Baptist church in America. He secured a charter (1644) for his R.I. colony which became a haven for oppressed people. The first Jews in New England were welcomed by Williams to settle at Providence.

WILLKIE, WENDELL LEWIS

Born: Feb. 18, 1892, Elwood, Ind. Died: Oct. 8, 1944, New York City. Graduated, Indiana U., B.S. (1913), LL.B. (1916). Admitted to bar and practiced in Ohio (1914-23) and New York City (1923-33).

Wendell L. Willkie was a progressive Republican businessman who ran for President against Franklin Roosevelt in 1940. He was head of the Commonwealth and Southern Corp., a utility company (1933-40), and had had no political experience. But he had political appeal and was swept into the nomination as his followers chanted, "We want Willkie!" Despite a strenuous campaign, he was defeated by Roosevelt's successful bid for a third term.

WILSON, JAMES

Born: Sept. 14, 1742, near St. Andrews, Scotland. Died: Aug. 21, 1798, Edenton, N.C. Attended Glasgow U. and Edinburgh U. (1757-63). To America (1766). Studied law and admitted to bar (1767). Continental Congress (1775). Congress of Confederation (1782-83, 1785-87). Associate justice of the U.S. Supreme Court (1789-98).

James Wilson, one of the leading lawyers of colonial times, supported the American Revolution and was a major contributor to the U.S. Constitution. He was a signer of the Declaration of Independence and was among the Pa. delegates to the Constitutional Convention (1787). He also helped draw up the Pa. constitution in 1790.

WILSON, WOODROW

Born: Dec. 28, 1856, Staunton, Va. Died: Feb. 3, 1924, Washington, D.C. Graduated, Princeton (1879). Studied law at U. of Virginia (1880). Admitted to the bar (1881). Taught history at Bryn Mawr (1885-88) and Wesleyan

Woodrow Wilson

(1888-90). *Professor, Princeton (1890-1902), and president (1902-10). Governor of N.J. (1911-13). Nobel peace prize (1919).*

Woodrow Wilson, twenty-seventh President of the U.S. (1913-21), was a famous educator and lawyer before his election to America's highest office. However, he is chiefly remembered for his idealistic approach to the duties of the presidency.

Wilson's election (1912) came in a time of turmoil; after he took office, World War I broke out in Europe. Wilson tried valiantly to keep the U.S. neutral, so that the nation could settle its internal problems and its difficulties with Mexico. The torpedoing of the steamship *Lusitania* (1915) by German submarines made that stand difficult. The episode caused the loss of 114 American lives and aroused much anti-German sentiment. Although Wilson avoided war at that point, the continuance later of unrestricted German submarine warfare finally forced him, on April 2, 1917, to ask Congress for a war declaration against Germany. He explained then that the U.S. must join the struggle "for the ultimate peace of the world and for the liberation of its peoples...." "We must make the world safe for democracy," he said. Four days later (April 6, 1917) Congress declared war.

Unfortunately, Wilson's greatness as a President lay more in his ability to envision the need for world unity than in his ability to effect it. On January 8, 1918, Wilson outlined for Congress Fourteen Points which he thought necessary to world peace. Most important among them was his plan for "a League of Nations... to safeguard the world against future war...." When the war ended (November 11, 1918), Wilson carried his grand design to the peace conference in Paris (December, 1918), but the treaty that resulted was disappointing to him and all his hopes had to rest on the plan for the League. This was later rejected by the U.S. Senate, along with the treaty of peace agreed to by Wilson.

After an unsuccessful attempt to gain popular support in America for the League, Wilson fell ill. He left the White House defeated and disillusioned, having failed to attain his dream of a world organization dedicated to maintaining peace.

WINTHROP, JOHN

Born: Jan. 22, 1588, Edwardstone, Suffolk, England. Died: Mar. 26, 1649, Boston, Mass. Attended Trinity Coll., Cambridge.

John Winthrop, a distinguished English lawyer who was a Puritan, practiced for fifteen years in London until chosen to be the Massachusetts Bay Colony's first governor (1629).

He arrived in Salem, Mass. (1630), with 700

John Winthrop

Thomas Wolfe

fellow Puritans. The newcomers settled at the present site of Boston, and prospered under Winthrop's leadership. He was governor until 1633 and again 1637-40, 1642-44, and 1646-49. For a total of ten years, he served as deputy governor. For purposes of defense against hostile Indians, Winthrop proposed a New England Confederation. When it was formed (1643), he became its president. Winthrop's *The History of New England from 1630-1649* was published in two volumes (1825-26).

WITHERSPOON, JOHN

Born: Feb. 5, 1723, near Edinburgh, Scotland. Died: Nov. 15, 1794, near Princeton, N.J. Graduated, U. of Edinburgh (1743). Ordained Presbyterian minister (1745). Member, Continental Congress (1776-82). Member, N.J. legislature (1783, 1789).

John Witherspoon came to America (1768) after accepting appointment as president of the Coll. of New Jersey (now Princeton). A believer in personal and religious liberty, Witherspoon was active in the American Revolution and signed the Declaration of Independence. He helped further the growth of the Presbyterian Church in the U.S. (1785-89), and is also noted for coining the word "Americanism," which appeared in an article he wrote on language for the *Pennsylvania Journal* (1781).

Frank W. Woolworth

WOLFE, THOMAS

Born: 1900, Asheville, N.C. Died: Sept. 15, 1938, Baltimore, Md. Graduated, U. of North Carolina (1920). Attended Harvard. Taught English, New York U. (1924-30).

In 1929 Thomas Wolfe published his first novel, *Look Homeward Angel*. A second novel, and sequel to the first, *Of Time and the River*, appeared in 1935. Both were Gargantuan efforts in which Wolfe made full use of an extraordinary memory of his past to create the characters and effects he wanted in his writings. He was attacked by some for formless and awkward writing. Others, however, defended his work as a unique contribution to American letters.

Wolfe's untimely death at the age of thirty-eight cut his writing career short. But three more novels, *The Web and the Rock* (1939), *You Can't Go Home Again* (1940), and *The Hills Beyond* (1941), were edited and published posthumously.

WOOD, GRANT

Born: Feb. 13, 1892, Anamosa, Ia. Died: 1942. Studied, Art Institute, Chicago (1912-14), and in Paris (1920-22).

Grant Wood was noted for his stylized and carefully painted pictures of the American scene. He began his art career as a teacher in a Cedar Rapids, Ia., public school. From 1935-42, he was artist-in-residence at the U. of Iowa. His best-known painting is *American Gothic* (1933). Others include *Woman with Plants* (1929) and *Daughters of Revolution* (1932).

WOOLWORTH, FRANK WINFIELD

Born: Apr. 13, 1852, Rodman, N.Y. Died: Aug. 8, 1919, Glen Cove, Long Island, N.Y.

Frank Woolworth was the originator of the five-and-ten-cent store. He opened his first one, which failed, in Utica, N.Y., in 1879. His second one opened at Lancaster, Pa., later the same year and succeeded. By 1911 there were over 1,000 "5 and 10's" in the U.S. and Canada.

The Woolworth building, for many years the world's tallest skyscraper (792 feet), was built in New York City in 1913.

Frank Lloyd Wright

WRIGHT, FRANK LLOYD

Born: June 8, 1869, Richland Center, Wis. Died: Apr. 10, 1959, Phoenix, Ariz. Studied civil engineering, U. of Wisconsin (1884-88).

Frank Lloyd Wright was one of America's foremost innovators in architecture. A disciple of Louis Sullivan, who taught that "form follows function," Wright carried Sullivan's principle one step further to develop his own theory of "organic" design. There should be a unity, he said, among the many particulars which affect a building's final appearance: the building's form, its function, the materials of which it is constructed, and the site on which it stands.

Besides his innovations in the field of architecture, Wright also founded and headed a cultural experiment at his home at Spring Green, Wis. There the Taliesin fellowship permitted bright young architects to live and work together under the master. They studied not only the technical aspects of architecture, but other arts as well.

Among Wright's works are Taliesin at Spring Green, Wis. (1911), the Imperial Hotel, Tokyo (1916-22), Suntop Homes, Ardmore, Pa. (1939), and the Guggenheim Museum, N.Y. (1959).

WRIGHT, ORVILLE

Born: Aug. 19, 1871, and Died: Jan. 30, 1948, Dayton, Ohio.

WRIGHT, WILBUR

Born: Apr. 16, 1867, Millville, near New Castle, Ind. Died: May 30, 1912, Dayton, Ohio.

Orville and Wilbur Wright launched mankind into the air age in 1903 with the first successful flights in a powered, piloted airplane. The Wright brothers were interested in the nearly unknown science of aeronautics from boyhood. They were excellent mechanics and constructed their first aircraft at their bicycle repair shop in Dayton (1892-1904).

After many experiments, they attempted a powered flight at Kitty Hawk, N.C., a seacoast location chosen (with the help of the U.S. Weather Bureau) because of its helpful air currents. On December 17, 1903, with Orville at the controls, their craft soared some 120 feet in twelve seconds. On their fourth flight, Wilbur stayed aloft for fifty-nine seconds while traveling 852 feet.

The Wright brothers improved their machine and by 1905 were able to fly a distance of twenty-four miles in thirty-eight minutes. They patented their airplane (1906) and established the Wright Co. to build it in quantity in 1909.

George Wythe

Orville (left) and Wilbur Wright

WYTHE, GEORGE

Born: 1726, Elizabeth Co., Va. Died: 1806, Richmond, Va. Attended William and Mary; read law; admitted to bar (1747). Member, Va. House of Burgesses (1754-55, 1758-68); clerk (1769-75). Continental Congress (1775-76). Judge, Va. chancery court (1778-1806). Teacher of law, William and Mary (1779-90).

George Wythe *(With)* was a signer of the Declaration of Independence (1776) and a Va. delegate to the Constitutional Convention (1787). Perhaps his chief importance, however, was as a teacher of law. He was one of the leading legal scholars of colonial times and numbered among his students John Marshall, Thomas Jefferson, James Monroe, Henry Clay.

Y

YOUNG, BRIGHAM

Born: June 1, 1801, Whitingham, Vt. Died: Aug. 29, 1877, Salt Lake City, Utah.

Brigham Young converted to the Mormon faith in 1832. He spent the rest of his life in its service. Upon the death of the original Mormon leader, Joseph Smith (1805-44), Young became president of the sect, officially known as the Church of Jesus Christ of Latter-Day Saints. When the Mormons were perse-

Brigham Young

cuted and expelled from Ill., Young led his followers on a migration across the plains to Utah (1846-47). On the shore of the Great Salt Lake, they settled, founding Salt Lake City (1847). Young was governor of the Utah Territory (1850-57).

In accordance with Mormon belief, Young practiced polygamy (marriage to more than one mate). At his death he had twenty wives and fifty-six children.

Z

ZANE, EBENEZER

Born: Oct. 7, 1747, near Moorefield, Va. (now W. Va.). Died: 1812, Wheeling, W. Va.

Ebenezer Zane was a pioneer who established the first permanent Ohio river settlement at Wheeling (1769) and founded Zanesville, Ohio (1799). He and his family successfully defended Fort Henry, near Wheeling, against Indian attacks during the American Revolution. In 1796, with congressional approval, he blazed a trail from Ohio to Ken. which in time became one of the important highways of the American West.

ZENGER, JOHN PETER

Born: About 1697, Germany. Died: July 28, 1746, New York City.

John Peter Zenger, publisher of the N.Y. *Weekly Journal,* was arrested by British colonial authorities in 1734. His paper had carried articles attacking the provincial governor, William Cosby, for certain political abuses. Zenger was charged with libeling (defaming) the governor and with sedition (stirring up discontent against the government). He was imprisoned for ten months before being brought to trial.

Zenger was defended by the great Andrew Hamilton (1676-1741), of Philadelphia, who argued that the press must be free to print the truth. The jury dismissed the libel charge and acquitted Zenger of sedition.

ZWORYKIN, VLADIMIR KOSMA

Born: July 30, 1889, Mourom, Russia. Graduated, Petrograd Institute of Technology (1912). Emigrated to U.S. (1916); naturalized citizen (1924). Graduated, U. of Pittsburgh, Ph.D. (1926). Research engineer, Westinghouse Co. (1920-29). Director, electronic research, Radio Corp. of America (1929-42, 1946-54). Honorary vice-president, R.C.A. (from 1954).

Vladimir Zworykin (Zwor-i-kin) invented two of the principal elements of present-day television: the "iconoscope" (the picture-transmitting tube of the TV camera) and the "kinescope" (the cathode-ray receiving tube). In 1933, using these two elements, he completed the first successful television transmission between New York City and Philadelphia.

He is currently engaged in research in medical electronics—the application of electronic science to medical problems.

CREDITS

The following sources are repeated frequently and, therefore, are referred to in the list below by the initials preceding their names.

CP—Culver Pictures
JH—John Hancock Mutual Insurance Co.
UPI—United Press International
NY—New York Public Library

VOLUME 11

Page 7—J. Adams: Harvard University. 8-9—J. Q. Adams: U.S. Department of State. S. Adams: JH. Addams: CP. Agassiz: NY. 10-11—Alger: JH. Allen and B. Arnold: NY. Altgeld and Anthony: CP. 12-13—H. Arnold: U. S. Air Force. Audubon: American Museum of Natural History. Bainbridge: New-York Historical Society. Barnum: JH. 14-15—Barton and Bell: JH. Beaumont: Wyeth Laboratories, Phila. Beebe: UPI. Beecher: NY. 16-17—Bennett: CP. Benton and Blaine: NY. 18-19—Boone, Bowditch, and Brady: JH. 20—Bryant: CP. Buchanan: NY.

Pages 22-3—Bunche and Bush: UPI. Burbank and Byrd: JH. 24-5—Carnegie: UPI. Carpenter: National Aeronautics and Space Administration. 26—Carson: CP. 28-9—Clemens: NY. Clinton: Independence Hall. 30-1—Cohn and Compton: UPI. Colt: CP. Coolidge and J. F. Cooper: New-York Historical Society. 32—P. Cooper: Cooper Union. 34-5—Custer: Library of Congress. 36-7—Debs: UPI. Decatur (ship): Mariner's Museum, Newport News, Va. Decatur: NY. Dickinson: Amherst College.

Page 39—Douglas: CP. 40-1—Dreiser: CP. Edison JH. 42-3—Edwards: NY. Einstein: JH. Eisenhower: U. S. Army. 44-5—Emerson: JH.Ericsson: NY. Farragut: Wadsworth Atheneum. 46-7—Faulkner: UPI. Field and Fillmore: CP. 48-9—Fitzgerald: UPI. Ford: JH. 50-1—Franklin: JH. Frémont: NY. 52-3—Fulton: Independence Hall. Garfield: Library of Congress. Garland: CP. 55—Gershwin: JH. Glenn: National Aeronautics and Space Administration. 56—Goddard: JH. 58-9—Grant: JH. Greeley: NY. 60-1—Greene: Independence Hall. Griffith: UPI. Grissom: National Aeronautics and Space Administration. Hale: New-York Historical Society.

Pages 62-3—Hamilton: NY. Hancock: JH. Hand: UPI. 64-5—Harper and J. C. Harris: CP. Harte: NY. 66—Hawthorne: CP. Hayes: Library of Congress. 68-9—J. Henry: American Philosophical Society. P. Henry: Independence Hall. Holmes, Sr.: Wyeth Laboratories, Phila. 70-1—Holmes, Jr.: UPI. Hopkins: CP. 72-3—Houston: Texas State Capitol (photo by Ellison, Austin). Howe: CP. Hughes: JH. 74-5—Hull: UPI. Irving: NY. 76-7—Jackson: Daughters of the American Revolution. The White House. Henry James: CP. William James: Harvard University. 78-9—Jay: Metropolitan Museum of Art. Jefferson: NY. Jones: Independence Hall. 80-1—Kane: New-York Historical Society. Keller: UPI. Kellogg: Wide World Photos. 82-3—Kettering: UPI. Key: J.H. 84-5—LaGuardia and Langmuir: UPI. Lake: CP.

VOLUME 12

Pages 86-7—Lardner: UPI. Latrobe: Maryland Historical Society. The White House. Lawrence: U.S. Naval Academy. 88-9—R. E. Lee, and Lewis and Clark: JH. LeMay: U.S. Air Force. J. L. Lewis: United Mine Workers. 90-1—Lincoln: Chicago Historical Society. Lindbergh: National Air Museum, Smithsonian Institution. Livingston: New-York Historical Society. Longfellow: NY.

Page 97—MacArthur: U.S. Army. 98-9—McCormick: JH. MacDowell: CP. 100-1—McGuffey: CP. D. Madison: New-York Historical Society. Mann: JH. 102—G. C. Marshall: U.S. Army. 104—Melville and Mencken: CP. 106-7—Mitchell: JH. Moody: CP. 108—D. Morgan: CP. 110-1—R. Morris and Morton: JH. Morse: NY. 112-3—Nast: NY. Nation: CP. Nimitz: U.S. Navy. 114-5—O'Neill: UPI. E. Otis: CP. J. Otis: NY. Paine: Marian Maurice. 116-7—Parkman and Patton: JH. Peale: Pennsylvania Academy of Fine Arts.

Pages 118-9—Peary: JH. M. C. Perry: U.S. Naval Academy. 120-1—Pershing: U.S. Army. Pierce: New-York Historical Society. Pike: Missouri Historical Society. 122-3—Pinkerton and W. S. Porter: CP. Poe: New-York Historical Society. Polk: NY. 124-5—Prescott, Pulitzer, and Pullman: CP. Rabi: UPI. 126-7—Randolph: CP. Reed: JH. 128-9—Remington and Revere: JH. 130-1—Riley: NY. Rittenhouse: American Philosophical Society. 132-3—Rockefeller, Roebling, and Rogers: NY. 134-5—Eleanor and Franklin Roosevelt: UPI. T. Roosevelt: JH. 136-7—Root: U.S. Department of State. Rosenwald: UPI. B. Ross: CP. 138-9—Royce: NY. Rush: Independence Hall. Ryder: CP. 140-1—Saint-Gaudens: Metropolitan Museum of Art. Salk: UPI. Schirra: National Aeronautics and Space Administration. 142-3—Schurz, Scott, and Sequoyah: NY. Seaborg: UPI. 144-5—Shepard: National Aeronautics and Space Administration. Sheridan: CP. Sherman: Yale University. 146-7—A. Smith: UPI. Sousa: NY. Spaatz: U.S. Air Force. 148-9—Stanford and Steffens: CP.

Pages 150-1—Steinbeck: UPI. Steinmetz: JH. 152-3—T. Stevens: CP. Stevenson: UPI. Stimson: U.S. Army. 154-5—Stowe, Sullivan, and Sumner: CP. Stuart: New-York Historical Society. 156-7—R. Taft and D. Taylor: UPI. W. H. Taft and Tarkington: CP. 158-9—Z. Taylor: NY. Tesla: CP. Thoreau: JH. 160-1—Thurber: UPI. Truman: Democratic National Committee. 162-3—Trumbull: CP. Tyler: The White House. Van Buren: NY. Vandenberg: UPI. 164-5—Vanderbilt and Veblen: CP. Wagner: UPI. Wainwright: U.S. Army. 166-7—Wald and L. Wallace: CP. H. Wallace and Warren: UPI. 168-9—B. T. Washington: CP. G. Washington: JH. 170-1—Wayne: CP. D. Webster: U.S. Department of State. N. Webster: JH. 172—West: Smithsonian Institution. Whistler: CP. 174-5—Whitman and Whitney: JH. Whittier: NY. 176-7—Willard: CP. Willkie: UPI. W. Wilson: JH. 178-9—Winthrop: CP. Wolfe: UPI. Woolworth: JH. 180-1—F. L. Wright: UPI. Wythe: NY. Wright Brothers: JH. 182—Young: CP.